print magic
decorating with stamps

print magic
decorating with stamps

stewart and sally walton

photography by graham rae

southwater

This edition is published by Southwater

Southwater is an imprint of Anness Publishing Ltd
Hermes House, 88–89 Blackfriars Road, London SE1 8HA
tel. 020 7401 2077; fax 020 7633 9499; info@anness.com

© Anness Publishing Ltd 1996, 2002

Published in the USA by Southwater, Anness Publishing Inc.
27 West 20th Street, New York, NY 10011; fax 212 807 6813

This edition distributed in the UK by The Manning Partnership
251–253 London Road East, Batheaston, Bath BA1 7RL
tel. 01225 852 727; fax 01225 852 852; sales@manning-partnership.co.uk

This edition distributed in the USA by National Book Network
4720 Boston Way, Lanham, MD 20706
tel. 301 459 3366; fax 301 459 1705; www.nbnbooks.com

This edition distributed in Canada by General Publishing
895 Don Mills Road, 400–402 Park Centre, Toronto, Ontario M3C 1W3
tel. 416 445 3333; fax 416 445 5991; www.genpub.com

This edition distributed in Australia by Sandstone Publishing
Unit 1, 360 Norton Street, Leichhardt, New South Wales 2040
tel. 02 9560 7888; fax 02 9560 7488; sales@sandstonepublishing.com.au

This edition distributed in New Zealand by The Five Mile Press (NZ) Ltd
PO Box 33-1071 Takapuna, Unit 11/101-111 Diana Drive, Glenfield, Auckland 10
tel. (09) 444 4144; fax (09) 444 4518; fivemilenz@clear.net.nz

A CIP catalogue record for this book is available from the British Library.

Publisher: Joanna Lorenz
Senior editor: Lindsay Porter
Project editor: Sarah Ainley
Photographer: Graham Rae
Designer: Bobbie Colgate Stone
Stylists: Diana Civil, Andrea Spencer and Fanny Ward

Previously published as *Stamp Decorating*

1 3 5 7 9 10 8 6 4 2

CONTENTS

INTRODUCTION

EVERY NOW AND THEN THERE IS A BREAKTHROUGH IN INTERIOR DECORATING — SOMETHING NEW CAPTURES THE IMAGINATION. STAMPING IS DEFINITELY ONE SUCH BREAKTHROUGH — IT IS ONE OF THE MOST INSTANT AND INNOVATIVE DECORATING TECHNIQUES AVAILABLE. WONDERFULLY SIMPLE YET STUNNINGLY EFFECTIVE, STAMPED DESIGNS CAN BE USED TO TRANSFORM ANYTHING FROM ENTIRE WALLS TO SHEETS OF GIFTWRAP; TO CREATE A THEME FOR A WHOLE ROOM OR TO PROVIDE ORIGINAL ACCESSORIES FOR AN EYE-CATCHING DISPLAY.

THE STAMP DECORATING IDEA COMES FROM THE RUBBER OFFICE STAMP AND IT USES THE SAME PRINCIPLE — ALL THE EQUIPMENT YOU WILL NEED IS A STAMP AND SOME COLOUR. COMMERCIAL STAMPS ARE READILY AVAILABLE, BUT INCLUDED IN THIS BOOK IS PRACTICAL ADVICE ON HOW TO CREATE YOUR OWN STAMPS FROM WOOD OR SPONGE, RUBBER OR LINOLEUM — ALMOST ANY MATERIAL THAT WILL HOLD COLOUR AND RELEASE IT. STAMPS CAN BE USED WITH AN INK PAD, BUT A SMALL FOAM ROLLER GIVES A BETTER EFFECT: JUST COAT THE STAMP WITH INK OR ORDINARY HOUSEHOLD PAINT — THIS MAKES STAMPING A FAIRLY INEXPENSIVE OPTION AND GIVES YOU A WIDE RANGE OF COLOURS TO CHOOSE FROM. FOLLOW THE TIPS ON APPLICATION TECHNIQUES AND PAINT EFFECTS TO ACHIEVE THE LOOK BEST SUITED TO YOUR HOME.

OVER 40 STYLISH DECORATING IDEAS ARE FEATURED IN THIS BOOK, BEAUTIFULLY PHOTOGRAPHED WITH CLEAR STEP-BY-STEP INSTRUCTIONS. YOU ARE SURE TO PROGRESS ON TO YOUR OWN PROJECTS ONCE YOU HAVE MASTERED THE BASIC TECHNIQUES — TRANSFORMING INTERIORS HAS NEVER BEEN SO TEMPTINGLY EASY.

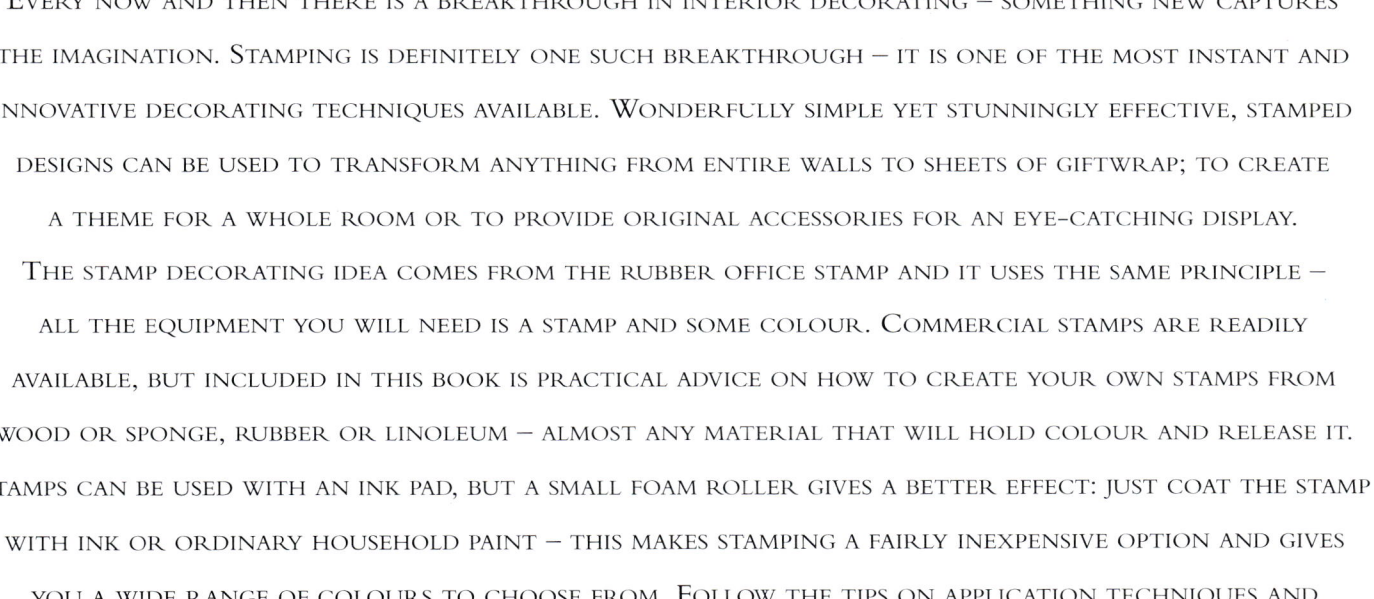
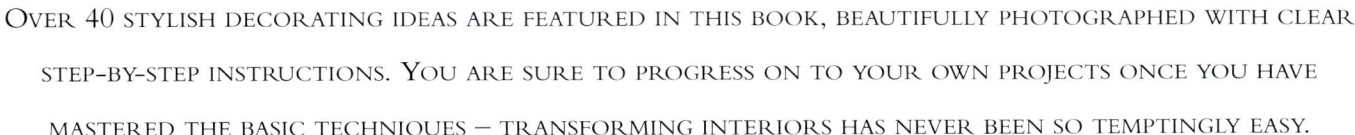

CREATING STAMPS

WOOD AND LINO STAMPS

Stamped prints were first made with carved wooden blocks. Indian textiles are still produced by hand in this way and it has recently become possible to buy traditional carved printing blocks.

Designs are cut in outline and the backgrounds are scooped out to leave the pattern shapes standing proud of the surface. Ink is applied, either by dipping the block or rolling colour on to the surface. The design is stamped and appears in reverse. The craft of making wooden printing blocks takes time to learn: you need special tools that are razor sharp, and an understanding about cutting with or against the grain. Practise on a bonded wood like marine plywood, which is relatively easy to carve.

Lino blocks are available from art and craft suppliers and usually come ready mounted in a range of sizes. Lino is a natural material made from ground cork and linseed oil on a webbed string backing. It is cut in the same way as wood, but has a less resistant texture and no grain to contend with, so is simple to cut.

To make a lino stamp you will need to trace a design and reverse the tracing before transferring it to the lino; this way you will print the design the right way around. Fill in all the background areas with a permanent marker pen: these are the parts to be scooped out, leaving the design proud of the surface. You will need a minimum of three tools - a scalpel, a "V"-shaped gouge and a scoop. All the tools should be kept as sharp as possible to make cutting easier and safer. Lino is easiest to cut when slightly warm, so place the block on a radiator for ten minutes before cutting. Hold the block with your spare hand behind your cutting hand, then if the tool slips you will not hurt yourself.

FOAM STAMPS

Different types of foam are characterized by their density. The main types used for stamp-making in this book are: high-density foam, such as upholstery foam; medium-density sponge, such as a kitchen sponge; and low-density sponge, such as a bath sponge. The different densities of foam are each suited to a particular kind of project; on the whole, medium- or low-density sponges are best for bold solid shapes, and high-density foam for fine details. Polystyrene foam can also be used but must be mounted on to hardboard. When the glue has dried, the polystyrene can be cut through to

▲ *Create the effect of wood blocks (top) with handmade lino cuts (bottom).*

There are two methods of creating your own rubber stamps. The first is to design on paper and then have a rubber-stamp company make one for you. This is worth doing if you intend to make good use of the stamp, and not just use it for a small, one-off project. Custom-made stamps are quite expensive to produce, so unless money is no object you may like to consider a second option. You can also make stamps by carving your design into an ordinary eraser. Many erasers are now made of a plastic compound instead of actual rubber, but the surface is smooth and easy to cut into. Two projects in this book, the tea service and personalized stationery, show you how to transfer and cut a pattern, and then print from a homemade rubber stamp.

▲ *Homemade stamps cut from high- and medium-density foam.*

▼ *Commercial rubber stamps are available in designs to suit all tastes.*

the board and the background can be lifted, leaving the design as a stamp.

To make a sponge stamp, first trace your chosen design then lightly spray the back of the pattern with adhesive, which will make it tacky but removable. Stick the pattern on to the foam and use a sharp scalpel to cut around the shape. Remove any background by cutting across to meet the outlines. If you are using medium- or low-density sponge, part it after the initial outline cut, then cut right through to the other side. High-density foam can be cut into and carved out in finer detail, it is also less absorbent, so you get a smoother, less textured print. If you are stamping over a large area, it is easier to mount the foam on to a

hardboard base and use wood glue to attach a small wooden door knob to the back, as a handle.

RUBBER STAMPS

Rubber stamps have come out of the office and playroom and emerged as remarkable interior decorating tools. Shops have sprung up dealing exclusively in an incredible range of stamp designs and the mail-order selections are astounding. The advantage of these pre-cut stamps is that you are instantly ready to transform fabric, furniture, even walls – and there can be no quicker way to add pattern to a surface. However, rubber stamps are most suited to small projects that require fine detail.

CREATING STAMPS

JACOBEAN POLYSTYRENE FLOWER

Polystyrene is easy to cut and gives good, clean edges. Always mount the polystyrene on hardboard before you cut your pattern.

YOU WILL NEED
- ♦ *sheet of polystyrene foam, approximately 1cm/½in thick*
- ♦ *piece of hardboard, the same size as the polystyrene*
- ♦ *wood glue or PVA glue*
- ♦ *felt-tipped pen*
- ♦ *scalpel*

1 Stick the sheet of polystyrene and hardboard backing together with wood glue or PVA glue.

2 Without waiting for the glue to set, draw the design using a felt-tipped pen. Remember that the pattern will reverse when printed.

3 Cut around the outline of the design using a scalpel. If this is done before the glue has set, these pieces will pull away easily.

4 Cut the edging details, removing unwanted pieces as you go.

5 Make shallow, angular cuts and scoop out the pattern details of the design. Use a new blade for this so that the cuts are sharp and you do not accidentally lift adjoining particles that have been only partially separated.

GEOMETRIC BORDER DESIGN

This border stamp is made from high-density foam. A good quality upholstery foam is recommended. The piece used here was sold by a camping supply shop for use as a portable, compact mattress.

YOU WILL NEED
◆ *wood glue or PVA glue*
◆ *high-density foam, such as upholstery foam, cut to the size of your design*
◆ *hardboard, cut to the same size*
◆ *felt-tipped pen*
◆ *ruler*
◆ *scalpel*
◆ *wooden block, for the handle*

1 Stick the foam on to the hardboard by applying wood glue or PVA glue to the rough side.

2 Without waiting for the glue to set, draw the pattern on to the foam using a felt-tipped pen and ruler. Use a scalpel to outline the sections to be cut away, then lift them out. If the glue is still tacky, this will be much easier.

3 Finally, using wood glue or PVA glue, stick the wooden block in the middle of the stamp back, to act as a handle. Allow to dry thoroughly.

SQUIGGLE FOAM STAMP

Foam comes in all shapes, sizes and densities. Make a visit to a specialist foam dealer, as inspiration for new ideas often springs from the discovery of new materials. Here is an idea for making a squiggle stamp in an original way.

YOU WILL NEED
◆ *masking tape*
◆ *length of cylindrical foam, about 2cm/¾in in diameter*
◆ *wood glue or PVA glue*
◆ *hardboard*

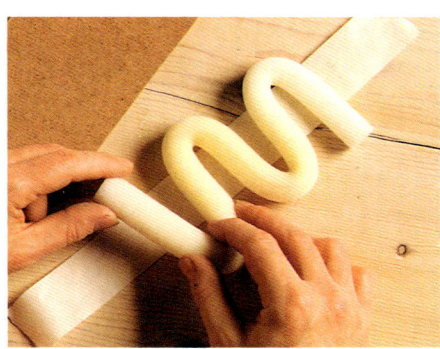

1 Lay out a length of masking tape, sticky side up. Twist the foam into a squiggle shape, pressing it on to the middle section of the tape.

2 Apply wood glue or PVA glue to the untaped side of the foam and turn it face-down on to the hardboard. Fold the tape ends under the hardboard to hold the foam in place while the glue sets. When dry, peel off the masking tape.

FLORAL LINOCUT

Cutting lino is a simple technique to master. You will be delighted with the intricacy of the motifs you can create using this medium.

YOU WILL NEED
- ◆ *tracing paper*
- ◆ *pencil*
- ◆ *sheet of transfer paper*
- ◆ *lino block*
- ◆ *masking tape*
- ◆ *scalpel*
- ◆ *lino-cutting tools: a "V"-shaped gouge and a "U"-shaped scoop*

1 Make a tracing of your chosen motif, the same size as the lino block. Slip a sheet of transfer paper (chalky side down) between the tracing and the lino, then tape the edges with masking tape.

2 Draw over the pattern lines with a sharp pencil. The tracing will appear on the lino block.

3 Remove the paper and cut around the outline with a scalpel. Cut any fine detail or straight lines by making shallow, angular cuts from each side, then scoop out the "V"-shaped sections.

4 Cut the rest of the pattern using the lino tools - the scoop for removing large areas of background, and the gouge for cutting the finer curves and pattern details. Hold the lino down firmly, with your spare hand placed behind your cutting hand to avoid accidents.

POTATO PRINT SUNBURST

Most of us learn the technique of using potatoes for printing as very young schoolchildren. Potato prints are amazingly effective, and should not be overlooked by adults.

YOU WILL NEED
- ◆ *medium-sized raw potato*
- ◆ *sharp kitchen knife*
- ◆ *fine felt-tipped pen*
- ◆ *scalpel*

1 Use a kitchen knife to make a single cut right through the potato. This will give the smoothest surface.

2 Draw the motif on to the potato with a fine felt-tipped pen. Remember that motifs reverse when stamped, although with the sunburst motif used here it will make no difference.

3 Use a scalpel to cut the outline, then undercut and scoop out the background. Potato stamps will not last longer than a few hours before they deteriorate, so keep a tracing of your motif if your project cannot be completed in one go. The design can then be re-cut using a fresh potato.

Basic Application Techniques

Stamping is a simple and direct way of making a print. The variations, such as they are, come from the way in which the stamp is inked and the type of surface to which it is applied. The stamps used in the projects were inked with a foam roller which is easy to do and gives reliable results, but each application technique has its own character. It is a good idea to experiment and find the method and effect that you most prefer.

INKING WITH A BRUSH

The advantage of this technique is that you can see where the colour has been applied. This method is quite time-consuming, so use it for smaller projects. It is ideal for inking an intricate stamp with more than one colour.

INKING WITH A FOAM ROLLER

This is the very best method for stamping large areas, such as walls. The stamp is evenly inked and you can see where the colour has been applied. Variations in the strength of printing can be achieved by only re-inking the stamp after several printings.

INKING ON A STAMP PAD

This is the traditional way to ink rubber stamps, which are less porous than foam stamps. The method suits small projects, particularly printing on paper. Stamp pads are more expensive to use than paint but are less messy, and will produce very crisp prints.

INKING BY DIPPING IN PAINT

Spread a thin layer of paint on to a flat plate and dip the stamp into it This is the quickest way of stamping large decorating projects. As you cannot see how much paint the stamp is picking up, you will need to experiment.

INKING WITH FABRIC PAINT

Spread a thin layer of fabric paint on to a flat plate and dip the stamp into it. Fabric paints are quite sticky and any excess paint is more likely to be taken up in the fabric rather than to spread around the edges. Fabric paint can also be applied by brush or foam roller, and is available with integral applicators from specialist outlets .

INKING WITH SEVERAL COLOURS

A brush is the preferred option when using more than one colour on a stamp. It allows greater accuracy than a foam roller because you can see exactly where you are putting the colour. Two-colour stamping is very effective for giving a shadow effect or a decorative pattern.

SURFACE APPLICATIONS

The surface on to which you stamp your design will greatly influence the finished effect.
Below are just some of the effects that can be achieved.

STAMPING ON ROUGH PLASTER

You can roughen your walls before stamping by mixing filler to a fairly loose consistency and spreading it randomly on the wall. When dry, roughen with coarse sandpaper, using random strokes.

STAMPING ON SMOOTH PLASTER OR LINING PAPER

Ink the stamp with a small foam roller for the crispest print. You can create perfect repeats by re-inking with every print, whereas making several prints between inkings varies the strength of the prints and is more in keeping with hand-printing.

STAMPING ON WOOD

Rub down the surface of any wood to give the paint a better "key" to adhere to. Some woods are very porous and absorb paint, but you can intensify the colour by over-printing later. If you stamp wood lightly the grain will show through. Seal your design with clear matt varnish.

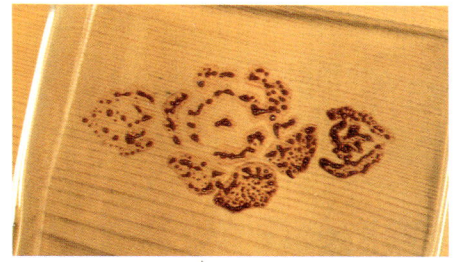

STAMPING ON GLASS

Wash glass in hot water and detergent to remove any dirt or grease and dry thoroughly. It is best to stamp on glass for non-food uses, such as vases. Ink the stamp with a foam roller and practise on a spare sheet of glass. As glass has a slippery, non-porous surface, you need to apply the stamp with a direct on/off movement. Each print will have a slightly different character, and the glass's transparency allows the pattern to be viewed from all sides.

STAMPING ON TILES

Wash and dry glazed tiles thoroughly before stamping. If the tiles are already on the wall, avoid stamping in areas which require a lot of cleaning. The paint will only withstand a gentle wipe with a damp cloth. Loose tiles can be baked to add strength and permanence to the paint. Read the paint manufacturer's instructions (and disclaimers!) before you do this. Ink the stamp with a small foam roller and apply with a direct on/off movement.

STAMPING ON FABRIC

As a rule, natural fabrics are the most absorbent, but to judge the stamped effect experiment on a small sample. Fabric paints come in a range of colours, but to obtain the subtler shades you may need to combine the primaries with black or white. Always place a sheet of card behind the fabric to protect your work surface. Apply the fabric paint with a foam roller, brush or by dipping. You will need more paint than for a wall surface, as fabric absorbs the paint more.

PAINT EFFECTS

Once you have mastered the basics of stamp decorating, there are other techniques that you can use to enrich the patterns and add variety. Stamped patterns can be glazed over, rubbed back or over-printed to inject subtle or dramatic character changes.

STAMPING EMULSION ON PLASTER, DISTRESSED WITH TINTED VARNISH

The stamped pattern will already have picked up the irregularities of the wall surface and, if you re-ink after several prints, some prints will look more faded than others. To give the appearance of old hand-blocked wallpaper, paint over the whole surface with a ready-mixed antiquing varnish. You can also add colour to a varnish, but never mix a water-based product with a spirit-based one.

STAMPING EMULSION ON PLASTER, COLOURED WITH TINTED VARNISH

If the stamped prints have dried to a brighter or duller shade than you had hoped for, you can apply a coat of coloured varnish. It is possible to buy ready-mixed colour-tinted varnish or you can add colour to a clear varnish base. A blue tint will change a red into purple, a red will change yellow into orange, and so on. The colour changes are gentle because the background changes at the same time.

STAMPING WITH WALLPAPER PASTE, PVA GLUE AND WATERCOLOUR PAINT

Mix three parts pre-mixed wallpaper paste with one part PVA glue and add watercolours. These come ready-mixed in bottles with integral droppers. The colours are intense so you may only need a few drops. The combination gives a sticky substance which the stamp picks up well and which clings to the wall without drips. The PVA glue dries clear to give a bright, glazed finish.

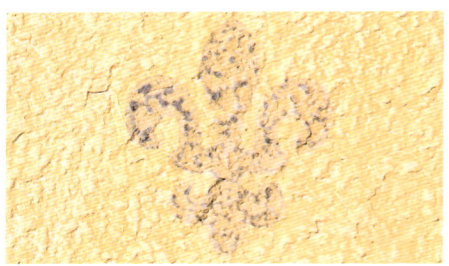

STAMPING WITH A MIXTURE OF WALLPAPER PASTE AND EMULSION

Mix up some wallpaper paste and add one part to two parts emulsion. This mixture makes a thicker print that is less opaque than the usual emulsion version. It also has a glazed surface that picks up the light.

STAMPING EMULSION ON PLASTER, WITH A SHADOW EFFECT

Applying even pressure gives a flat, regular print. By pressing down more firmly on one side of the stamp you can create a shadow effect on one edge. This is most effective if you repeat the procedure, placing the emphasis on the same side each time.

STAMPING A DROPPED SHADOW EFFECT

To make a pattern appear three-dimensional, stamp each pattern twice. Make the first print in a dark colour that shows up well against a mid-tone background. For the second print, move the stamp slightly to one side and use a lighter colour.

DESIGNING WITH STAMPS

To design the pattern of stamps, you need to find a compromise between printing totally at random and measuring precisely to achieve a machine-printed regularity. To do this, you can use the stamp block itself to give you a means of measuring your pattern, or try strips of paper, squares of card and lengths of string. Try using a stamp pad on scrap paper to plan your design but always wash and dry the stamp before proceeding to the main event.

USING PAPER CUT-OUTS

The easiest way to plan your design is to stamp and cut out as many pattern elements as you need and use them to mark the position of your finished stamped prints.

CREATING A REPEAT PATTERN

Use a strip of paper as a measuring device for repeat patterns. Cut the strip the length of one row of the pattern. Use the stamp block to mark where each print will go, with equal spaces in between. You could mark up a vertical strip. Position the horizontal strip against this as you print.

USING A PAPER SPACING DEVICE

This method is very simple. Decide on the distance between prints and cut a strip of paper to that size. Each time you stamp, place the strip against the edge of the previous print and line up the edge of the block with the other side of the strip. Use a longer strip to measure the distance required.

CREATING AN IRREGULAR PATTERN

If your design doesn't fit into a regular grid, plan the pattern first on paper. Cut out paper shapes to represent the spaces and use these to position the finished pattern. Alternatively, raise a motif above the previous one by stamping above a strip of card positioned on the baseline.

DEVISING A LARGER MOTIF

Use the stamps in groups to make up a larger design. Try stamping four together in a block, or partially overlapping an edge so that only a section of the stamp is shown. Use the stamps upside down, back to back and rotated in different ways. Experiment on scrap paper first.

USING A PLUMBLINE

Attach a plumbline at ceiling height to hang down the wall. Hold a card square behind the plumbline so that the string cuts through two opposite corners. Mark all four points, then move the card square down. Continue in this way to make a grid for stamping a regular pattern.

Kitchens

Considering the effort and financial outlay involved in replacing a kitchen, stamp decorating seems a particularly attractive option when you find that you simply cannot bear your existing kitchen any longer. Stamping allows you creative free-rein, dependant only on your imagination and the amount of time you have available; whether your kitchen is in need of a complete new image or just a little vamping-up, the extent of the changes you make is entirely up to you. Experiment with commercial and home-made stamps, with colours and designs, to find the look best suited to your home.

*S*CANDINAVIAN KITCHEN

Replacing a kitchen is one of the major financial outlays facing a home-owner, and also a major disruption. It often involves waiting a long time for your dream kitchen while you put up with an outdated and intensely disliked one.
This project will revitalize and update your existing kitchen so that you may well stop pining for that refit altogether. The most time-consuming part of the project is painting the cupboards and walls white, but once you've done that, you can stamp on the heart pattern that really rings the changes.
Don't worry if you've got melamine cupboards, as they can be cleaned to remove any grease and then painted with an oil-based matt paint such as eggshell or satinwood. If your units are white, but very clinical, you can brighten them up by adding red wooden handles to match the hearts.
Start this project on a Saturday morning and you could have a new-look kitchen by the end of the weekend.

YOU WILL NEED
thick card
scissors
red emulsion paint
plate
foam roller
small and large heart stamps
kitchen paper
ruler
pencil
clear matt varnish and brush (optional)
red and white gingham curtains
backing paper (such as thin card or newspaper)
fabric paint in pink and white
iron

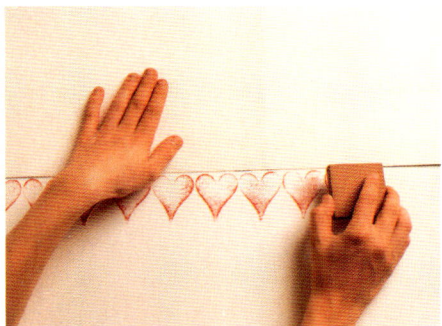

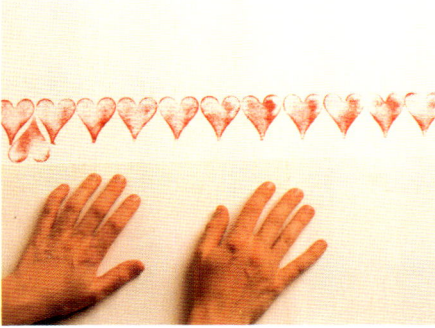

1 Cut a square of thick card, approximately 30x30cm/12x12in. To stamp the top frieze, hold the card square against the wall with the top edge resting against the ceiling. Assuming that the ceiling is at a right angle to the wall, this will give you a straight line to follow. Otherwise, you will need to make adjustments visually.

Spread some red paint on to the plate and run the roller through it until it is evenly coated. Ink the small stamp and begin printing in the lefthand corner. Butt the edge of the stamp block up against the card square and print a close row of hearts.

2 Print the first heart in the second row with the point facing up. Then align the card square with the bottom of the print and hold it in place so that you keep a straight line along the row.

3 To print the frieze above the work surface, first cut out a piece of thick card the width of the desired gap between the work surface and the border. Place this against the wall, resting on the work surface, and rest the base of the stamp block on it.

Ink the large stamp with red paint and then blot it before stamping so that the print is very light and airy.

4 Ink the small stamp and print a row of upside-down hearts between the large hearts.

5 To print the cupboards, use a ruler and pencil to mark the centre point of each cupboard door.

6 Ink the large stamp and print one heart above the centre point and one below so that the points face inwards.

7 Ink the small stamp and print a heart either side of the centre point with the points facing inwards. The cupboard doors can be protected by applying a coat of varnish.

8 To print the curtains, protect your work surface with a large sheet of paper and spread the fabric over this. Put the curtains on some backing paper on a work surface.

9 Spread some pink fabric paint on to the plate and run the roller through it until it is evenly coated. Ink the small stamp and print pink hearts down the side edges with two red squares between each one.

10 Stamp pink hearts across the fabric, counting six red squares between the points on the first row. Then begin the second row six squares down and three across. Repeat these two rows to cover both the curtains.

11 Ink the large stamp with white fabric paint, then over-print all the pink hearts. Fix the fabric paint with a hot iron following the manufacturer's instructions.

HEART PELMET

This pelmet co-ordinates nicely with the kitchen project, but you could equally well try it in another room. Pelmets add depth to windows and they are very easy to make. Attach a wooden shelf to the top of the window frame. Cut the front and side pieces from hardboard and hammer them in place with panel pins. A jigsaw is useful for cutting a scalloped edge, but a straight edge looks just as good.

YOU WILL NEED
emulsion paint in white and red
paintbrush
plate
foam roller
trellis heart stamp

1 Paint the pelmet white and leave to dry. Spread some red paint on to the plate and run the roller through it until it is evenly coated

2 Ink the stamp and begin printing at one end of the front board. Use only half of the stamp for the first print so that the other half can be printed on the side piece to make the design wrap round the corner. Aim to make these prints as symmetrical as possible.

3 Stamp one heart in each scallop (if you have them); otherwise stamp them at equal distances along the length of the pelmet.

WINDOW BOX

Galvanized iron has staged a comeback recently and it is definitely here to stay.
Although many of the everyday objects around the home are now mass-produced in plastic,
you just can't beat the look of iron alternatives.
The individuality of the window box in this project will enhance any window ledge. The three
hearts were stamped with acrylic paint to make it just that bit more special. Plant it with flowers
and you've got a complete showpiece!

YOU WILL NEED
galvanized iron window box
ruler
pencil
red acrylic paint
plate
foam roller
small and trellis heart stamps

1 Clean the surface of the window box. Using a ruler, mark the centre point with a pencil.

2 Spread some red paint on to the plate and run the roller through it until it is evenly coated. Ink the small stamp and print a heart at the centre.

3 Ink the trellis stamp with the red paint and make a print either side of the small heart.

COUNTRY KITCHEN

Specialist suppliers sell beautifully decorated tiles but they can be very expensive. So why not use stamps and paint to make your own set of exclusive tiles? The grape stamp is inked with two shades of green that blend in the middle in a slightly different way each time. Small touches such as the rustic hanging rail and the wooden plate add rustic authenticity to a country kitchen. The wood for the rail needs to be old and weathered. The nails banged into the rail as hangers are called "cut" nails, which are used for floorboarding. Attach the rail to the wall and hang fresh herbs from it, conveniently close to the cooker. The wooden plate is stamped with different parts of the tendril motif to make a decorative border and central design.

YOU WILL NEED
plain tiles
clean cloths
acrylic enamel paint in blue-green and
yellow-green
plates
foam rollers
grape, leaf and tendril stamps
olive-green emulsion or acrylic paint
scrap paper
weathered piece of wood, maximum
30cm/12in long
long cut nails or hooks
hammer or drill
black stamp pad
scissors
wooden plate, sanded to remove any
stain or varnish
vegetable oil

1 Wash the tiles in hot water and detergent, then wipe dry to ensure that there is no grease on the surface.

2 Spread some blue-green acrylic enamel paint on to one plate and some yellow-green on to another. Run the rollers through the paint until they are evenly coated.

3 Ink the leaf, the top and the right side of the grape stamp with the blue-green roller. Ink the rest of the stamp with the yellow-green roller.

4 Stamp a bunch of grapes in the centre of each tile. Remove the stamp directly, taking care not to smudge the print. If you do make a mistake, wipe off the paint with a clean cloth and start again. Follow the manufacturer's instructions to "fire" the tiles in the oven if required.

5 For the hanging rail, spread some olive-green emulsion paint on to a plate and run a roller through it until it is evenly coated. Ink the leaf stamp and stamp twice on to scrap paper to remove some of the paint.

6 Stamp on to the length of weathered wood without re-inking the stamp. The resulting print will be light and faded-looking, like the wood itself. Make as many prints as you can fit along the length. Hammer in the nails or drill and screw in the hooks to complete the hanging rail.

7 For the wooden plate, stamp several tendrils on to scrap paper and cut them out. Arrange them on the plate to work out the spacing and positioning of the motifs.

8 Spread some olive-green emulsion or acrylic paint on to a plate and run the roller through it until it is evenly coated. Ink the corner of the tendril stamp comprising the two curls that will make up the border pattern and carefully begin stamping around the edge of the plate.

9 Ink the whole stamp and stamp two tendrils in the centre of the plate. Leave to dry.

10 Dip a clean cloth into some vegetable oil and rub this into the whole surface of the plate, including the stamped pattern. You can repeat this process once all the oil has been absorbed into the wood. Each time you rub oil into the plate, the colour of the wood will deepen.

FOLK COFFEE CANISTER

Rescue an old kitchen canister and give it a new identity as a piece of folk art. Painted tinware was tremendously popular with the early American settlers, and pedlars roamed the countryside loaded with brightly painted cans, jugs and bowls that they sold from door to door. All these years later they are still a popular way of brightening up kitchen shelves. Prepare the canister by rubbing down the old paint with sandpaper to provide a key for a fresh coat of emulsion paint. After stamping, bring out the colour and protect the surface with several coats of clear varnish.

YOU WILL NEED
kitchen canister
sandpaper
emulsion paint in brick-red, black and bright red
fine artist's paintbrushes
plates
foam roller
tulip stamp
clear gloss varnish and brush

1 Rub back the canister with sandpaper. Paint the canister and lid with brick-red emulsion. Leave to dry, then paint the rim of the lid black.

2 Run the roller through the black paint until it is evenly coated. Ink the tulip stamp and print a tulip on the side of the canister, tilting the stamp block around the curve of the canister.

3 Fill in the tulip using bright red paint and a fine paintbrush.

4 Apply several coats of gloss varnish to seal and protect the canister. Leave each coat to dry completely before applying the next.

VINE LEAF CUTLERY RACK

A small wooden cutlery rack like this one provides another ideal surface for stamping. Use the stamps to loosely co-ordinate your kitchen or dining room without being swamped by matching patterns and colours. The wood has been stained blue and is then rubbed back to reveal some of the natural grain underneath. The two colours of the pattern are stamped separately using thinned emulsion for a light and airy finish.

YOU WILL NEED
wooden cutlery rack, stained blue
fine sandpaper
emulsion or acrylic paint in dark and light
olive-green
plate
foam roller
leaf stamp

1 Sand the surface of the cutlery rack to reveal some of the grain. Spread some dark olive-green paint on to a plate and thin it with water to a runny consistency.

2 Use the roller to ink the leaf stamp. Print two leaves side by side on the back and front of the rack and two leaves one above the other on the sides. Leave to dry.

3 Spread some light olive-green paint on to a plate and run the roller through it until it is evenly coated. Ink just the tips of the leaves and overprint all the darker green prints. If some of the prints are slightly off-register, this will only add to the rustic appearance of the rack.

CANDLE BOX

A long time ago every home would have had a candle box hanging on the kitchen wall, kept full to meet the lighting needs of the household. Although rarely needed in quite the same way today, candle boxes are still popular, and add to a comfortable atmosphere. Candle boxes can be bought, but are quite easy to make from five pieces of wood. The open top allows you to see when your supply is running low and the sight of the new candles is somehow reassuring as well as attractive.

YOU WILL NEED
wooden candle box
fine-grade sandpaper
shellac and brush
plate
dark oak woodstain
foam roller
diamond, crown and fleur-de-lys stamps
lining brush

1 Sand away any varnish and smooth any rough edges on the box.

2 Paint the bare wood with a single coat of shellac.

3 Spread some woodstain on to a plate and run the roller through it until it is evenly coated. Ink the stamps and print a single motif on each side of the box. Print the fleur-de-lys so it will be visible above the candles. Use the lining brush to paint a thin border on all sides.

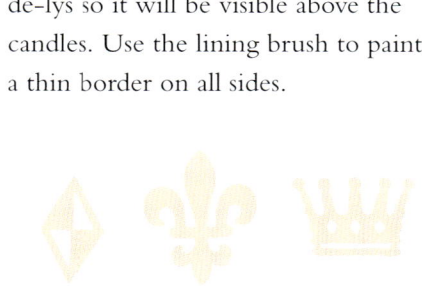

BEACH-COMBER'S STOOL

If you stumble across a small milking stool like this one, don't hesitate, just buy it! These sorts of stools were, and still are, used in kitchens, gardens and worksheds for a whole range of tasks. Small children love to sit on them and adults find them invaluable when shelves are just out of reach. They can be used for weeding, sketching, fishing or any activity that requires being close to the ground but not actually on it.

This junk shop find was painted orange before being stamped with the seashore pattern. It's just the thing to sit on while peeling prawns or cleaning mussels.

YOU WILL NEED
small wooden stool
orange emulsion paint
paintbrush
emulsion, acrylic or poster paint in deep
red, purple and pale peach
plate
foam roller
shell, seahorse and starfish stamps
matt varnish and brush

1 Paint the stool orange and leave to dry. Spread some deep red paint on to the plate and run the roller through it until it is evenly coated. Ink the shell stamp and make a print in the centre of the stool.

2 Ink the seahorse stamp with purple paint and make a print either side of the shell.

3 Ink the starfish stamp with pale peach paint. Print a starfish border, overlapping the edge so that the design goes down the sides of the stool.

4 When the paint has dried, apply a coat of varnish to the stool. This will dry to a matt sheen.

PROVENÇAL KITCHEN

This kitchen is a dazzling example of contrasting colours – the effect is almost electric. Colours opposite each other in the colour wheel give the most vibrant contrast and you could equally well experiment with a combination of blue and orange or red and green. If, however, these colours are just too vivid, then choose a gentler colour scheme with the same stamped pattern. The kitchen walls were colourwashed to give a mottled, patchy background. Put some wallpaper paste in the colourwash to make the job a lot easier – it also prevents too many streaks running down the walls. You can stamp your cupboards to co-ordinate with the walls.

YOU WILL NEED
emulsion paint in deep purple and pale yellow
wallpaper paste (made up according to the manufacturer's instructions)
paintbrush
plumbline
approx. 30 x 30cm/12 x 12in cardboard
pencil
plates
foam rollers
rosebud and small rose stamps
acrylic paint in red and green
clear matt varnish and brush

1 To make the colourwash, mix one part deep purple emulsion with one part wallpaper paste and four parts water. Make it up in multiples of six. It is best to make more than you need. Colourwash the walls. If runs occur, just pick them up with the brush and work them into the surrounding wall, aiming for a patchy, mottled effect.

2 Attach the plumbline at ceiling height, just in from the corner. Hold the cardboard square against the wall so that the string cuts through the top and bottom corners. Mark all four points with a pencil. Continue moving the square and marking points to make a grid pattern.

3 Spread some deep purple paint on to the plate and run the roller through it until it is evenly coated. Ink the stamp and print a rosebud on each pencil mark until you have covered the wall.

4 If you wish to create a dropped-shadow effect, clean the stamp and spread some pale yellow paint on to the plate. Ink the stamp and over-print each rosebud, moving the stamp so that it is slightly off-register.

5 Continue over-printing the rosebuds, judging by eye the position of the yellow prints.

6 For the cupboard doors, spread some green and red paint on to the plates and run the rollers through them until they are evenly coated. Ink the rose with red and the leaves with green. (If one colour mixes with the other, just wipe it off and re-ink.) Print a rose in the top lefthand corner.

7 Print the stamp horizontally and vertically to make a border along the edges of the door panel.

8 When you have printed round the whole border, leave the paint to dry. Apply a coat of varnish to protect the surface.

WOODEN WINE CRATE

Old wood usually looks best with a faded rather than freshly painted pattern. The grape design here does not detract from the crate's rustic quality because it has been stamped in a muted green, then rubbed back to blend with the existing lettering on the wood. If you are lucky enough to find a custom-made wine crate like this one, it will simply need a good scrubbing with soapy water, then be left to dry before you stamp it.

YOU WILL NEED
old wine crate or similar wooden box
scrubbing brush (optional)
olive-green emulsion paint
plate
foam roller
grape stamp
fine sandpaper

1 If necessary, scrub the crate well with soapy water and a scrubbing brush and leave it to dry.

2 Spread some olive-green emulsion paint on to a plate and run the roller through it until it is evenly coated. Ink the stamp and begin stamping a random pattern of grapes. Stamp at different angles to add variety.

3 Cover all the surfaces of the crate, overlapping the edge if the planks are too narrow to take the whole motif.

4 Leave the paint to dry, then rub back the pattern with sandpaper, so that it becomes faded and blends with the original surface decoration or lettering. Rub gently and aim for a patchy, distressed appearance.

GILDED TRAY

This simple wooden tea tray is transformed into an item of historic grandeur by using an easy gilding technique. Begin by sanding away any old paint or varnish and painting the base of the tray in black and the sides in red-ochre emulsion, applying two or three coats. The heraldic motifs make up a central panel design and the fine outline is repeated around the edge of the tray. The tray is stamped twice, first with the red-ochre and then with gold size, which is a transparent glue used for gilding. Dutch metal leaf is then applied over the size.

YOU WILL NEED
wooden tea tray, prepared as above
ruler
pencil
fleur-de-lys and diamond stamps
black stamp pad
scrap paper
scissors
emulsion paint in black and red-ochre
plates
foam roller
thin wooden batten
lining brush
gold size and Dutch metal leaf
soft and hard paintbrushes
shellac and brush

1 Measure out and mark in pencil the six-sided central panel. Draw a border around the edge of the tray. Print eight fleurs-de-lys and five diamonds on paper and cut them out. Use them to plan your design, marking the base point of each motif in pencil on the tray. Spread some red-ochre paint on to a plate and run the roller through it until it is evenly coated. Ink the stamps and print the fleur-de-lys and diamond pattern.

2 Using the batten to support your hand, use the lining brush and red-ochre emulsion to paint a fine line around the design, following the pencil lines of the central panel. Paint another fine line just inside the edge of the tray. If you have never used a lining brush, practise on scrap paper until you are confident.

3 Paint the sides of the tray with size. Leave the size to become tacky, according to the time specified by the manufacturer. Place one sheet of Dutch metal leaf on to the size at a time and burnish with the back of a soft brush. Spread the gold size on to a plate and use the roller to ink the stamps with size. Over-print the red-ochre patterns, stamping each print slightly down and to the left of the already printed motif to create a dropped shadow effect. Leave the size to become tacky and gild with Dutch metal leaf in the same way as before. Use a stiff brush to sweep away the excess leaf. Seal the whole tray with a protective coat of shellac.

ℬATHROOMS

THE BATHROOM IS OFTEN OVERLOOKED WHEN IT COMES TO HOME-DECORATING

BUT IN FACT THIS IS ONE OF THE ROOMS THAT BENEFITS THE MOST FROM

A THOROUGH BRIGHTENING-UP. A COMPLETE NEW IMAGE IS OFTEN

WHAT IS NEEDED HERE, AND BECAUSE BATHROOMS ARE USUALLY ONE OF THE

SMALLER ROOMS IN THE HOUSE, YOU CAN AFFORD TO BE THAT LITTLE BIT

MORE ADVENTUROUS. A CRITICAL LOOK AT YOUR BATHROOM WILL SHOW

YOU WHERE IMPROVEMENTS CAN BE MADE — FEATURES TO BE HIGHLIGHTED

AND PROBLEM AREAS TO BE DISGUISED. THE GREAT BONUS OF STAMPING IS

THAT YOU CAN PRINT ON ALMOST ANY SURFACE, MAKING IT INCREDIBLY

EASY TO BUILD A THEME AND ENTIRELY CHANGE THE FEEL OF YOUR BATHROOM.

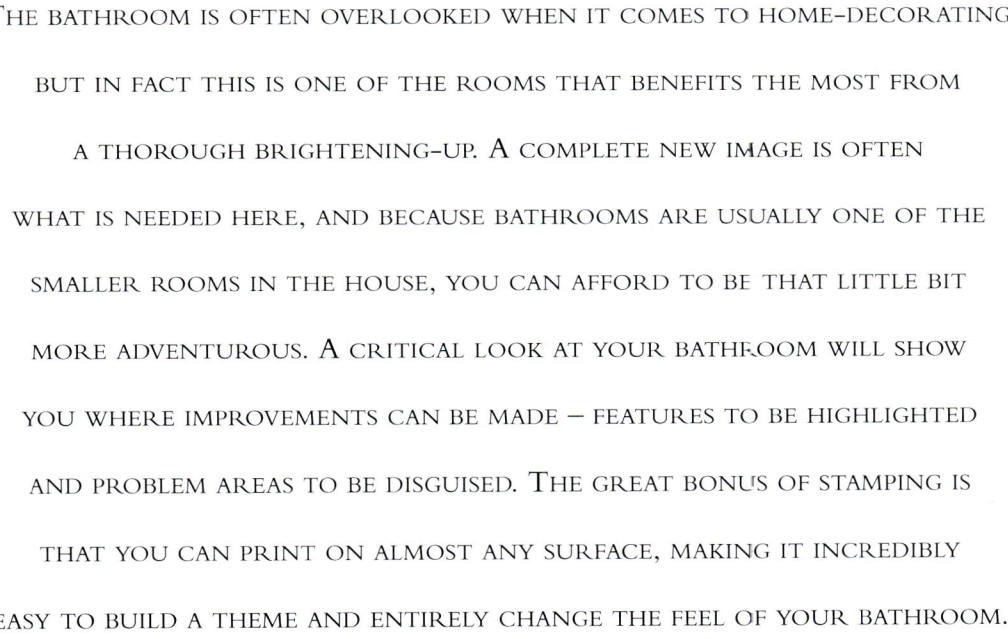

ＳTAR-STUDDED BATHROOM

Transform your bathroom into one fit for royalty or film stars in the space of a weekend. The cost
is minimal and the luxurious result is bound to impress all future bathers.
If you have an old bathroom, it is worth investigating the underside of the boxed–in bath – you
may be lucky enough to discover an old claw–footed iron bath like this one. However, the lack of
an elegant bath just adds to the challenge. You can paint the boarding and arrange it with drapes
to soften the edges.
Who could fail to feel pampered in such wonderful surroundings?

YOU WILL NEED
tapemeasure
small semi-circular wooden shelf
pelform (see step 1)
craft knife
ruler
pencil
piece of calico (see step 3)
gold fabric paint or PVA glue mixed
with bronze powder
plate
foam roller
large star stamp
gold tassel
PVA glue or needle and matching
sewing threads
length of muslin, for the curtains
iron-on hem fix
iron-on header tape
iron
backing paper (such as thin card or
newspaper)
staple gun and staples
drawing pins
round satin cushion
enamel paint or emulsion paint
metal primer
paintbrush

1 To make the pelmet, measure the curved edge of the shelf and cut the pelform to this length.

2 Using a ruler and pencil, draw a series of points along the bottom of the pelform. Cut them out.

3 Place the pelform over a rectangle of calico and cut around the shape, leaving a 3cm/1¼in seam allowance. Peel off the backing paper and smooth the fabric on to the pelform. Turn the piece over and snip into the corners. Then peel off the backing strip and stick the seams down.

4 Spread some gold fabric paint on to the plate and run the roller through it until it is evenly coated. Ink the stamp and print a row of stars across the middle of the pelmet. Glue or sew a tassel to each point. Now fix the shelf to the wall, about 30cm/12in from the ceiling, exactly halfway along the length of the bath. ▶

5 To make the curtains, cut the muslin into two pieces and turn up a seam at both ends using iron-on hem fix. Attach iron-on header tape to one end of each curtain. Lay out one of the curtains on backing paper. Spread some gold fabric paint on to the plate and run the roller through it until it is evenly coated. Ink the stamp and print a widely spaced row of stars across the bottom of the fabric.

6 Print another row of stars to fall between the stars in the first row. Repeat these rows to cover the curtain. Stamp the second curtain in the same way.

7 Gather up the curtains by pulling the header tape string. Staple the curtains to the shelf.

8 Attach the pelmet to the shelf using drawing pins.

9 To make the cushion, place a ruler diagonally across the cushion and make a small pencil mark in the centre. Check the position by intersecting the centre point from a different angle.

10 Spread some gold paint on to the plate and run the roller through it until it is evenly coated. Ink the stamp and print a single star in the centre of the cushion.

11 Paint the bath with a coat of metal primer, if necessary. Paint the bath or bath panel cream and leave to dry. Paint the legs gold. Spread some gold paint on to the plate and run the roller through it until it is evenly coated. Ink the large stamp and begin by printing the top row of stars. Continue stamping in the same way as for the curtains so that the stars fall between the spaces of the row above. Follow the curve of the bath.

REGAL BATHROOM

Decorating a bathroom on a budget usually means that all your money goes on the bathroom suite, flooring and taps. A pure white bathroom may look clean and fresh, but a certain amount of warmth in pattern and colour is needed to prevent it from seeming too clinical. Stamping enables you to achieve a co-ordinated finish on tiles, fabric and furniture at little extra cost. If you stamp a set of tiles using acrylic enamel paint before fixing them to the wall, the design can be baked in the oven for a very hardwearing finish. If the tiles are already in place, you can use the same paint but it won't stand up to abrasive cleaning, so use it away from sinks and baths.

YOU WILL NEED
masking tape
diamond and crown stamps
pencil
emulsion paint in grey and yellow-ochre
plates
foam rollers
wooden shelf with rail
PVA glue
clear matt varnish and brush
black stamp pad
scrap paper
scissors
white cotton piqué handtowels
grey fabric paint
iron
plain white tiles
clean cloth
grey acrylic enamel paint

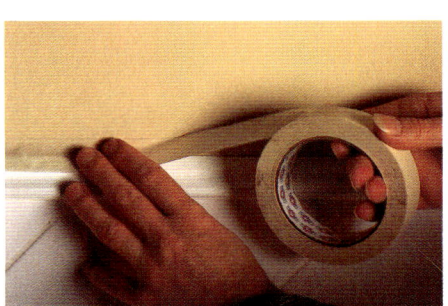

1 Stick a length of masking tape along the top edge of the the moulding above the tiles or along the top of the tiles themselves if there is no moulding. This will give you a straight line to stamp along. Mark the position of the actual stamp in pencil. on the edge of the stamp block.

2 Spread some grey emulsion paint on to a plate and run the roller through it until it is evenly coated. Ink the stamp and print the diamond border. Line up the pencil mark on the stamp block with the edge of the previous print so that diamonds meet without overlapping.

3 To decorate the shelf, mix two parts yellow-ochre emulsion paint with one part PVA glue. The glue will make the paint stickier and will dry to give a bright, glazed finish.

4 Run the roller through the paint until it is evenly coated and ink the diamond stamp. The design of the pattern will depend on the shelf. Here, a diamond is printed on each plank to make evenly spaced rows.

5 Stamp a crown in the centre at the top of the shelf with a diamond to either side.

6 Seal the shelf with at least one coat of clear matt varnish.

7 Use the stamp pad to print 20 diamond motifs on paper and cut them out. Arrange them in three rows across the width of a towel, adjusting the spacing until you are happy with it.

8 Remove the top two rows of the pattern, leaving only the bottom row in place. Spread some grey fabric paint on to a plate and run the roller through it until it is evenly coated. Ink the stamp and remove each paper diamond individually as you replace it with a stamped print.

9 Stamp the next row of the pattern with a diamond between each pair on the row below. Draw a central line on the back of the stamp block. Line it up with the top of the first row to help you position the second row.

10 Complete the border pattern with a third row of diamonds. Fix the fabric paint with a hot iron, following the manufacturer's instructions.

11 Wash the tiles with detergent and dry them well. Hold the tiles by their edges to avoid fingerprints, which will repel the paint.

12 Spread some grey acrylic enamel paint on to a plate and run the roller through it until it is evenly coated. Ink the crown stamp and print a single crown in the centre of each tile on the diagonal.

BLISSFUL BATHROOM

Sea-greens and turquoise-blues are ideal for the watery environment of a bathroom and the floaty mood can be enhanced by the addition of coloured muslin drapes or glass jars filled with foam bath. The walls are first colourwashed and then a cherub border is stamped in sea-green. When the border has dried, a tinted varnish is brushed on to protect it and add another watery dimension. The chair back is stamped in emulsion paint and then varnished in a different shade. The plain wooden cupboard is stamped with cherubs and rubbed back to give it an aged look.

YOU WILL NEED
emulsion paint in turquoise, cream,
sea-green and pale blue
wallpaper paste
household paintbrushes
plates
foam rollers
cherub and swag stamps
pencil (optional)
spirit level (optional)
small strip of card
clear water-based varnish and brush
sepia artist's watercolour
wooden kitchen chair with broad
back-rest
fine artist's paintbrush
wire wool
small wooden hall cupboard
fine-grade sandpaper
clean cloth

1 Paint the walls turquoise. Mix one part cream emulsion with one part wallpaper paste and four parts water. Using random brush-strokes, paint the walls. Spread some sea-green emulsion on to a plate and run a roller through it. Ink the first cherub stamp.

2 Rest the base of the stamp block on the top edge of the rail or tiles, or use a pencil and spirit level to mark a line as a guide. Print a row of cherubs, alternating the two stamps and using a card strip to space the border. Tint the varnish with artist's watercolour and brush it over the whole wall.

3 To stamp the chair, first paint it sea-green and leave to dry. Spread some turquoise emulsion paint on to a plate and mix in some cream paint to lighten the shade. Run a roller through the paint until it is evenly coated. Ink the swag stamp and print a swag in the centre of the chair back.

4 Lighten the sea-green paint further with cream and add hand-painted detail to the stamped swag with a fine paintbrush. Leave to dry. Rub back the paint with wire wool to simulate natural wear and tear. Apply a coat of clear varnish.

5 To stamp the cupboard, first paint it in pale blue emulsion paint. Before it has dried, rub back the paint with a clean cloth so that the pale blue colour stays in the grain, but much of the wood is revealed.

6 Rub back the paint with fine-grade sandpaper to reveal some more of the wood underneath.

7 Spread some sea-green emulsion paint on to a plate and run the roller through it until it is evenly coated. Ink both cherub stamps and make two prints on the door panel. Leave to dry.

8 Lightly rub back the cherub stamps with a cloth to give an antique look.

SUN-BLEACHED BATHROOM

It's hard to beat the freshness of pure, white bathroom walls, but they can look rather clinical and stark if left completely plain. This project is an ideal compromise and leaves the walls looking sun-bleached and bright.

The walls are stamped with a widely spaced pattern of yellow-ochre seashore shapes. One of the joys of stamping is creating a unique design which distinguishes your decor from ready-made wallpaper or tiles. Here the stamps are rotated with each new print to give a pleasingly random pattern.

To achieve the sun-bleached look, give the walls an all-over light wash with watered-down white emulsion. All the sharp contrasts disappear to give a calming, peaceful finish.

YOU WILL NEED
emulsion paint in yellow-ochre and white
plate
foam roller
shell, starfish and seahorse stamps
paintbrush
white cotton fabric, for the basin curtain
iron-on seam fix
iron
backing paper (such as thin card or newspaper)
thin card spacer, 2.5 x 15cm/1 x 6in
cobalt-blue fabric paint
curtain header tape
double-sided strong tape
unbleached calico, 1½ times the window width, plus required drop
scrap paper
eyelet kit
hammer
thick cord, 1½ times the window width

1 Spread some yellow-ochre paint on to the plate and run the roller through it until it is evenly coated. Ink the shell stamp and make a print anywhere on the wall.

2 Rotate the stamp and print another shell about two hand-widths from the first one. Ink the starfish stamp and add this motif to the pattern.

3 Ink the seahorse stamp and use it to fill in the spaces to complete the pattern. Continue working until all the walls are covered.

4 Mix about six parts water with one part white emulsion and brush this wash over the entire wall to achieve the sun-bleached effect.

5 To make the basin curtain, seam all edges of the fabric using iron-on seam fix. Protect your work surface with backing paper and lay the fabric over this. Place a thin strip of card along the top edge of the fabric to help space the prints for the border. Ink the seahorse stamp with cobalt–blue fabric paint and make the first print at one edge with the top of the stamp butting up against the card.

6 Continue stamping across the top, keeping the seahorses in a straight line and evenly spaced. If you do make a mistake, don't worry because the pleating will disguise it. Leave to dry.

7 Fix the fabric paint with a hot iron following the manufacturer's instructions. Cut a strip of curtain header tape to fit the width of the curtain. Stick the tape to the wrong side of the curtain, along the top row of the seahorses.

8 Stick the double-sided tape along the edge of the basin, allowing enough room above it for the ruffled top of the curtain. Begin gathering the curtain by pulling the two cords.

9 If necessary, readjust the cords to make even gathers. Use the double-sided tape to secure the edge of the curtain to the basin. Work your way around the basin, so the curtain hangs evenly, with equal gathers along the width.

10 To make the window curtains, seam all edges of the fabric using iron-on seam fix. Protect your work surface with backing paper and lay the fabric over this. Ink the shell stamp with cobalt-blue fabric paint and make the first print in one corner of the curtain.

11 Rotate the stamp with each print and continue printing a random pattern. Use your hand between the shells to judge the distance between the prints.

12 Make sure that you print over the edges of the curtains in some places. Place a piece of scrap paper under the edge of the curtain to take up the ink from the overlapping stamp. Fix the fabric paint with a hot iron following the manufacturer's instructions.

13 Attach the eyelets to the top edge of the curtains, at least 10cm/4in apart.

14 Thread the cord through the eyelets from the back of the curtain to hang as shown on the right.

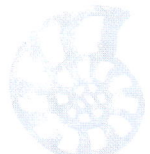

Starfish Bathroom Chair

Old wooden chairs are not expensive and, with a bit of careful hunting round second-hand shops, you should be able to find yourself a real bargain. Take the time to strip the old layers of paint - it might take some time, but it gives you a much better base to work on. This chair was given an undercoat of white emulsion, then it was dragged with yellow-ochre in the direction of the grain before being stamped in light grey. Choose colours that complement your bathroom scheme so that your Starfish Chair will blend in with existing fittings.

You will need
medium-grade sandpaper
wooden chair
emulsion paint in white, yellow-ochre and
light grey
paintbrush
plate
foam roller
starfish stamp
clear matt varnish and brush

1 Sand or strip the chair, then apply a coat of white emulsion. Mix a thin wash of about five parts water to one part yellow-ochre emulsion. Use a dry brush to drag a little glaze at a time in the direction of the grain. Keep drying the brush as you work, to ensure you do not apply too much glaze.

2 Spread some light grey paint on to the plate and run the roller through it until it is evenly coated. Ink the starfish stamp and print around the edge of the chair seat so that the design overlaps on to the sides.

3 Fill in the seat area with starfish stamps, rotating the stamp to a different angle after each print. Space the stamps quite close together to make a dense pattern. Leave to dry thoroughly before applying a coat of varnish to protect the surface.

Bedrooms

The great thing about decorating a bedroom is that you really do have *carte blanche* to do whatever you like. If you feel bound by convention with rooms that are more socially on view, you can really let yourself go with this one — after all, this is a place of relaxation and a room to be comfortable in. Make the look complete with a co-ordinated scheme, by using fabric inks to stamp a matching design on curtains, cushions and linen. Because decorating with stamps is relatively inexpensive and hassle-free, you can make your design as quirky as you like — if you tire of the style, simply paint over it and stamp something new.

COTTAGE BEDROOM

Stamp denim-blue roses on to an off-white background and decorate bed linen to match. If your walls are pristine and smooth, there are ways to create the effect of rough plaster. It may seem perverse to roughen up a nice, smooth wall, but there is nothing to compare with the character imparted by irregular plasterwork. The trick here is to scratch the walls to provide a "key" to work on and then to apply a coat of filler, varying the depths in places. Leave this to set, then rub some of it away before it has completely hardened – this will give a deep distressed look. Use a rasp and coarse sandpaper to roughen up the rest of the wall, and you will have created your own cottage walls.

YOU WILL NEED
emulsion paint in white, buttermilk-yellow
and denim-blue
large paintbrush
plumbline
approx. 30 x 30cm/12 x 12in cardboard
pencil
plate
foam roller
large rose, rosebud and small
rose stamps
royal blue fabric paint
scrap paper
scissors
plain white sheets
iron
backing paper (such as thin card or
newspaper)

1 Paint the walls white, then make a colourwash by mixing four parts water to one part buttermilk-yellow. Brush this on to the walls, using random, sweeping strokes. If runs occur, just pick them up with the brush and work them into the surrounding wall.

2 Attach the plumbline at ceiling height, just in from the corner. Hold the cardboard square against the wall so that the string cuts through the top and bottom corners. Mark all four points with a pencil. Continue moving the square and marking the points to make a grid pattern.

3 Spread some denim-blue paint on to the plate and run the roller through it until it is evenly coated. Ink the large rose stamp and print one rose on every pencil mark.

4 Ink the rosebud stamp and print between the large roses to complete the pattern.

5 For the sheets, spread some royal-blue paint on to the plate and run the roller through it until it is evenly coated. Ink the small rose stamp and make prints on the paper. They will be used to work out the spacing.

6 Cut out the rose prints from the paper. If you do not have enough to work out a complete pattern across the sheet, print some more.

7 Wash and iron the sheet prior to stamping to ensure the best prints.

8 Place the backing paper under the ironed sheet.

9 Position the paper cut-outs on the sheet, rearranging them until you are happy with the design. You could make an all-over pattern of staggered rows, or simply print a border along the top.

10 Ink the stamp with the roller, and print the roses, using the paper cut-outs as a guide. If you are printing a border, line up the sewn border edge against the top of the stamp block to keep the line straight.

11 Fix the fabric paint with a hot iron following the manufacturer's instructions.

Rose Cushions

Don't get your needle and thread out for this project – just buy plain cushion covers and stamp them with contrasting colours! New cushions revitalize existing decor and they can change the mood of a room in an instant. They are also a clever way to distribute a themed pattern round a room as they subtly reinforce the rosy look.

Natural fabrics like this thick cotton weave are perfect for stamping because they absorb the fabric paint easily to leave a good, sharp print. Fabric paints can be fixed with a hot iron after applying to ensure a long-lasting and hard-wearing finish.

You will need
backing paper (such as thin card or newspaper)
natural-fabric cushion covers in two different colours
fabric paint in white and blue
plate
foam roller
rosebud, large rose and small rose stamps
scrap paper
scissors
iron

1 Place the backing paper inside the darker cushion cover. Spread some of the white paint on to the plate and run the roller through it until it is evenly coated. Ink the rosebud stamp and make the first print in the bottom righthand corner of the cover.

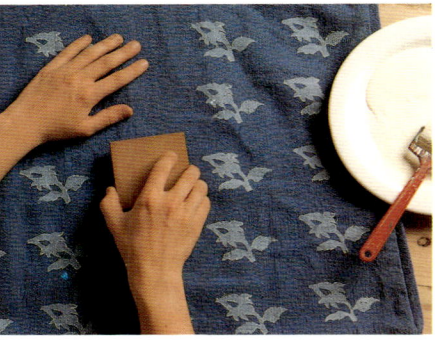

2 Continue stamping in rows, using the stamp block as a spacing guide – use the top edge as the position for the bottom edge of the next print. You should be able to judge it by eye after a couple of prints. Fill the cover with a grid pattern of rosebuds.

3 For the second cover, ink all three stamps with the blue paint. Stamp each one on to the paper and cut them out. Use the paper patterns to work out the position of the rows.

4 Re-ink the large rose stamp and make the first print in the top lefthand corner. Use the paper pattern to help with the spacing and complete the row.

5 Ink the small rose stamp and complete the next row, again using the paper pattern for spacing.

6 Use the rosebud stamp in the same way to complete the pattern. Finally, fix the fabric paints on both covers with a hot iron following the manufacturer's instructions.

LEAFY BEDROOM

This pretty bedroom is decorated using two very quick, easy and effective techniques. The stripes are applied first on to a white wall, using the same type of small foam roller as is used for inking the stamps. Rolling colour on in this way gives a mottled coverage with slightly wavy edges to give a subtle, faded look. The leaves are stamped in a diagonal in opposite directions to make a zigzag pattern. The leaf theme is extended to the round dressing-table box, which is completed with hand-painted brushstrokes.

YOU WILL NEED
wallpaper paste
emulsion paint in grey, leaf-green, deep blue-green, deep red and dusky pink
plates
spirit level
5 x 2.5cm/2 x 1in wooden batten
masking tape
foam rollers
medium square-tipped artist's brush
leaf stamp
round, lidded wooden box
fine lining brush
clear satin varnish and brush

1 Mix the wallpaper paste, then mix one part wallpaper paste with one part grey emulsion paint on a large plate. The mixture will produce a slightly translucent glaze when dry. Tape the spirit level to the wooden batten with masking tape.

2 Run a roller through the paint until it is evenly coated. Hold the batten-ruler in one corner of the wall and run the roller down its edge to the dado rail or skirting board. Line up the ruler with the edge of this stripe and continue rolling across the wall.

3 Using a paintbrush and grey paint, complete the stripes at the ceiling and dado rail or skirting board, where the roller has not reached.

4 Mix one part leaf-green emulsion paint with one part wallpaper paste on a plate and use to ink the leaf stamp. Stamp columns of leaves between the grey stripes. Stamp the leaves diagonally, changing the direction of the stamp to create a zigzag pattern.

5 Continue stamping until all the white stripes are filled. Re-ink the stamp when the print becomes very pale, but do allow some variety in the depth of colour of the prints. This irregularity will emphasize the feel of hand-blocked wallpaper.

6 For the dressing-table box, use deep blue-green emulsion to paint the box and lid and leave to dry. Spread some deep red paint on to a plate and run the roller through it until it is evenly coated. Ink the leaf stamp and stamp evenly spaced leaf motifs around the sides of the box.

7 Stamp two leaves in the centre of the box lid, side by side and facing in opposite directions. Use the square-tipped brush to paint a border around the top edge of the lid. Paint the sides of the lid in the same colour.

8 Using a fine lining brush and dusky pink emulsion, paint veins on the leaves and a fine line around the inside edge of the red border. Support your painting hand with your free hand as you work. You may need to practise the strokes on scrap paper first.

9 Leave the paint to dry, then seal the box with a coat of satin varnish.

STARRY BEDROOM

At first glance, this bedroom looks wallpapered, but a closer examination reveals the hand-printed irregularity of the star stamps – some are almost solid colour while others look very faded. This effect is achieved by making several prints before re-inking the stamp. The idea is to get away from the monotony of machine-printed wallpaper, where one motif is the exact replica of the next, and create the effect of exclusive, hand-blocked wallpaper at a fraction of the price. The grid for the stars is marked using a plumbline and pencil. If you haven't got a plumbline, make your own by tying a key to a piece of string. You're bound to be delighted with the final result, and feel a great sense of achievement at having done it all yourself.

YOU WILL NEED
sandy-yellow emulsion or distemper paint
large paintbrush
30 x 30cm / 12 x 12in card
plumbline
pencil
brick-red emulsion paint (matchpot size)
plate
foam roller
folk-art star stamp

1 Paint the walls sandy yellow with emulsion or distemper. You may prefer a smooth, even finish or areas of patchy colour – each will create its own distinct look.

2 Hold the card square diagonally against the wall in the corner at ceiling height. Attach the plumbline at ceiling height so that the string cuts through the top and bottom corners of the square. Mark all four points with a pencil. Continue moving the square and marking points to form a grid.

3 Spread some brick-red paint on to the plate and run the roller through it until it is evenly coated. Ink the stamp and print a star on every pencil mark, or line the block up against each pencil mark to find your position, whichever you find easiest.

4 Experiment with the stamp and paint to see how many prints you can make before re-inking. Don't make the contrast between the pale and dark too obvious or the eye will always be drawn to these areas.

SMALL CUPBOARD

A popular designer's trick is to paint a piece of furniture in the same colours as the background of the room, but in reverse. This co-ordinates the room without being overpoweringly repetitive. A small cupboard like the one in this project is perfect for such a treatment. Don't be too precise in your stamping – a fairly rough-and-ready technique gives the most pleasing results.

YOU WILL NEED
wooden cupboard
emulsion paint in brick-red and yellow
paintbrush
plate
foam roller
small star stamp
fine wire wool or sandpaper
water-based matt varnish and brush

1 Paint the cupboard with a base coat of brick-red emulsion.

2 Spread some yellow paint on to the plate and run the roller through it until it is evenly coated. Ink the stamp and print on to the cupboard.

3 Rub around the edges with wire wool or sandpaper to simulate natural wear and tear. This will give an aged appearance sympathetic to a country-style interior.

4 Apply a coat of varnish tinted with the brick-red paint (one part paint to five parts varnish) to tone down the contrast between the prints and the background paint.

CHERUB BEDROOM

This bedroom has been given a complete cherubic transformation but the use of a subtle, natural colour scheme has prevented the effect from being overwhelming. Earthy colours harmonize naturally to produce a restful atmosphere. The three-dimensional effect on the walls is achieved by stamping first in a darker shade and then slightly off-register in a lighter colour. The cherubs seem to float free of the wall surface, which is most fitting for these little winged beings. The muslin drapes hang from a semi-circular shelf above the bed to make a soft frame around the pillows. The cherubs are stamped in cream fabric paint to create a very delicate pattern.

YOU WILL NEED
plumbline
25 x 25cm/10 x 10in card
pencil
emulsion paint in terracotta and cream
plates
foam rollers
cherub and swag stamps
10m/11yd unbleached muslin
iron
scissors
needle and matching sewing thread
newspaper
strip of cardboard
pen
ruler
fabric paint in cream and terracotta
semicircular wooden shelf and
wall fixtures
staple gun and staples
two rough silk cushion covers
backing card
black stamp pad
scrap paper
tassels
two cushion pads
vase
clean cloth
terracotta acrylic enamel paint

1 Attach a plumbline at ceiling height, just in from one corner. Hold the card square against the wall so that the string cuts through the top and bottom corners. Mark all the corner points in pencil. Move the card to continue marking a grid for stamping.

2 Spread some terracotta emulsion paint on to a plate and run a roller through it until it is evenly coated. Use it to ink the first cherub stamp and make a print with the base of the stamp resting on one of the pencil marks. Cover the wall with cherubs, re-inking the stamp as necessary.

3 Clean and dry the stamp, then re-ink it with cream emulsion. Position the stamp slightly to the right and just above each terracotta cherub print to achieve a three-dimensional effect.

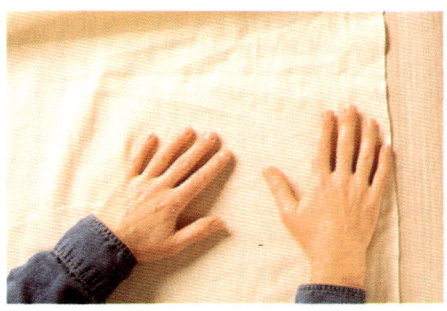

4 To make the drapes, wash and iron the muslin before use, then cut it into two 5m/5½yd pieces and hem the ends. Cover a table with newspaper and lay the muslin flat.

5 Make a spacer from a long strip of cardboard, by ruling lines across the strip at regular intervals. Spread some cream fabric paint on to a plate and run a roller through it until it is evenly coated. Ink the first cherub stamp and print a row across the muslin above alternate marks on the spacer.

6 Print the second row of cherubs to fall between those in the first row. Use the paper strip to maintain an even distance between the rows. Move the fabric down and continue stamping to cover the whole length. Stamp the second drape in the same way. Follow the manufacturer's instructions to fix the fabric paint with an iron.

7 Staple the drapes to the shelf so that they meet at the front. Attach the edges first, then pleat the muslin and staple each fold to the shelf. Insert the staples vertically so that they are hidden in the folds. Fix the shelf to the wall, centrally above the bed and at picture rail height. Allow the drapes to fall on either side of the bed and cascade on to the floor.

8 To make the cushions, insert the backing card inside the cushion covers and lay on a flat surface.

9 Use the stamp pad to print both cherub stamps on scrap paper. Arrange them on the cushion cover to plan your design.

10 Spread some terracotta fabric paint on to a plate and run a roller through it until it is evenly coated. Ink the cherub stamps and print on to the fabric, removing each paper motif as you stamp in its place. Follow the manufacturer's instructions to fix the fabric paint with an iron.

11 Sew tassels on to the corners of the cushion covers and insert the cushion pads.

12 To stamp the vase, first wash it in hot water and detergent, then wipe dry with a clean cloth to ensure that there is no grease on the surface.

13 Spread some terracotta acrylic enamel paint on to a plate. Run a roller through it until it is evenly coated and ink the swag stamp.

14 Stamp swags around the vase. Remove the stamp directly and take care that it does not slide on the smooth surface and smudge the print. If you do make a mistake, wipe off the paint with a clean cloth and start again. Follow the manufacturer's instructions to "fire" the vase in a domestic oven.

BEAUTIFUL BEDROOM

Who wouldn't want to sleep in this lavender-grey and white bedroom? The choice of two cool colours has a very calming effect. The frieze is stamped in white at dado height around a lavender-grey wall. The simple reversal of the wall colours on the headboard provides both contrast and continuity. You can stamp on to an existing headboard or make one quite simply from a sheet of MDF cut to the width of the bed. Use the stamps to make matching accessories in the same colours. Make the most of the stamps' versatility by using only the central part of the tendril stamp on the narrow border of a picture frame.

YOU WILL NEED
drawing pin
string
spirit level
emulsion paint in white and lavender-grey
plates
foam rollers
tendril, grape and leaf stamps
headboard or sheet of MDF painted white
masking tape
pencil
ruler
broad, square-tipped artist's paintbrush

1 Use a drawing pin to attach one end of the string in a corner of the room at dado height. Run the string along the wall to the next corner and secure the end. Check the string with a spirit level and adjust if necessary.

2 Spread some white emulsion paint on to a plate and run a roller through it until it is evenly coated. Ink all three stamps and stamp a tendril, grape and leaf in sequence along the wall. Align the top edge of each stamp with the string and print below it.

3 When the first wall is complete, move the string to the next wall and continue all the way around the room. To decorate the headboard, stick masking tape around the top and side edges of the white board.

4 Spread some lavender-grey paint on to a plate and run a roller through it until it is evenly coated. Ink the leaf and tendril stamps. Align the stamp block with the masking tape and stamp alternate leaves and tendrils down both sides of the board.

5 Ink all three stamps and stamp a tendril, grape and leaf along the top edge of the board. Repeat the sequence to complete the row. Check the spacing before you stamp – wide spacing is better than the motifs appearing squashed together.

6 Measure a central panel on the board and lightly draw it in pencil. Stick strips of masking tape around the panel and the border. Mix some lavender-grey and white paint, then paint the border and the central panel in this pale grey colour.

GRAPE JUG

A white ceramic jug like this one seems to be crying out for some stamped decoration, and the grapevine stamps do the trick in minutes. Choose a well-proportioned plain jug and transform it into something that is decorative as well as practical. Acrylic enamel paint is new on the market and, although it resembles ordinary enamel, it is in fact water-based and does not require harmful solvents for cleaning brushes and stamps. Follow the manufacturer's instructions to "fire" the stamped jug in a domestic oven to add strength and permanence to the pattern. Without "firing", the paint will only stand up to non-abrasive cleaning.

YOU WILL NEED
white ceramic jug
clean cloth
grape, tendril and leaf stamps
black stamp pad
scrap paper
scissors
acrylic enamel paint in black and
ultramarine blue
plate
foam roller

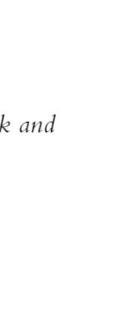

1 Wash the jug in hot water and detergent, then wipe dry to ensure that there is no grease on the surface.

2 Print a grape, a tendril and a leaf on to scrap paper and cut them out. Arrange them on the jug to plan the finished design.

3 Mix together the black and the blue acrylic enamel paint on a plate. Run the roller through the paint until it is evenly coated and ink the stamps. Stamp the motifs following your planned arrangement as a guide.

4 The leaf may be used to fill any gaps, or the pattern may be repeated on the other side. Follow the manufacturer's instructions if you wish to make the design permanent by "firing" in the oven.

COUNTRY GRANDEUR BEDROOM

Redecorating the bedroom can be as refreshing as taking a holiday, and stamping is such fun that it won't seem like work at all. First sponge over a cream background with terracotta emulsion and add a final highlight of pink to give a warm, mottled colour. Any plain light-coloured wall can be covered in this way. Two of the stamps are then combined to make a border which co-ordinates with an all-over pattern on the wall and a bedside table. You could go on to decorate matching curtains and cushions, or stamp a border on sheets and pillowcases.

YOU WILL NEED
emulsion paint in dark salmon-pink, off-white and dusky pink
plates
foam rollers
fleur-de-lys and diamond stamps
thin card
scissors
plumbline
pencil
long ruler
small table, painted off-white
pair of compasses
black stamp pad
scrap paper
paintbrush
clear matt varnish and brush

1 Spread some dark salmon-pink emulsion on to a plate and use the roller to ink the fleur-de-lys stamp. Stamp a row of fleurs-de-lys above the dado rail using a piece of card 7.5cm/ 3in wide to space the motifs.

2 Ink the diamond stamp with dark salmon-pink emulsion and print diamonds between the fleurs-de-lys. Use a card spacing device if you are not confident about judging the positioning by eye.

3 Cut a card square about 25 x 25cm/10 x 10in. Attach a plumbline at ceiling height, just in from one corner and so that the weighted end hangs down to the border. Use to mark a grid for the diamond stamps.

4 Ink the diamond stamp with salmon-pink emulsion and print a diamond on every pencil mark to make an all-over pattern.

5 Spread some off-white emulsion on to a plate and run the roller through it until it is evenly coated. Ink both stamps and over-print the border pattern. To create a dropped shadow effect, stamp each print slightly below and to the left of the motif that has already been printed.

6 Overprint the wall pattern in the same way.

7 Lay the ruler across the table top from corner to corner in both directions to find the central point. Mark the centre lightly in pencil.

8 Set the compasses to a radius of 10 cm/4in and lightly draw a circle in the centre of the table top.

9 Increase the radius to 12.5cm/ 5in. Position the point of the compasses on the edge of the circle, in line with the middle of the back edge of the table. Mark the point on the circle at the other end of the compasses, then move the point of the compasses to this mark. Continue around the circle to make five divisions. Join them lightly in pencil to give a pentagonal shape.

10 Use the stamp pad to print 15 diamonds on paper and cut them out. Arrange them around the pentagon, as shown. Use the compasses to mark the inner point of the five inward-pointing diamonds.

11 Spread some dusky pink emulsion on to a plate and run the roller through it until it is evenly coated. Ink the stamp and print the five inward-pointing diamonds at the marked positions.

12 Re-ink the stamp as necessary and print the rest of the medallion pattern. Print an arrangement of three diamonds in each corner of the table top. Paint any moulding and handles on the table in the same pink. Seal the table with a coat of clear matt varnish.

COTTAGE PLAY ROOM

Folk-art patterns really do suit all age groups and this playroom could easily be transformed into a teenager's room by removing the toys and replacing them with a desk and chair. The same bright colours appear on the walls and cushions to create a harmonious look. Dividing the wall horizontally makes the ceiling appear lower, which is ideal for a child's room. If the room has a dado rail, paint it ochre, otherwise divide the wall with a horizontal stripe. The cushion covers can be bought or made at home. They are stamped using special fabric paint, which can be heat-sealed with an iron following the manufacturer's instructions.

You will need
plumbline
25 x 25cm/10 x 10in card
pencil
emulsion paint in grey and deep brick-red
plates
foam rollers
pineapple, leaf and tulip stamps
two yellow floor cushions or 4m/4yd
yellow cotton fabric
iron
black stamp pad
scrap paper
scissors
fabric paint in ochre and dark brown
small pine milking stool or child's chair
fine sandpaper
fine artist's paintbrush
wire wool

1 Use the plumbline, card square and pencil to mark a grid for stamping the pineapple motif. Spread some grey paint on to a plate and use the roller to ink the pineapple stamp. Print a pineapple on each pencil mark.

2 Wash and press the cushion covers or fabric. Stamp 12 leaves on to scrap paper, cut them out and arrange on the cushions to plan the design of the prints. Then start to print the leaf motif with ochre fabric paint.

3 Ink the stamp with dark brown fabric paint and fill in the spaces. Use the roller to re-ink the stamp as you work, to maintain a dark colour. Seal the fabric paint with an iron following the manufacturer's instructions.

4 Rub down the top and edges of the stool or chair with sandpaper. Use the deep brick-red paint to print two tulips, end to end in the middle of the top of the stool. Paint a border just inside the top edge of the stool and leave to dry. Rub the paint back with wire wool to simulate wear and tear.

NURSERY WALLS

Children are often bombarded with a riot of primary colours or surrounded in pretty pastels, so this dark colour scheme provides an unusual and refreshing change. It gives the room a wonderful period feel and the deep blue-green shade is known for its calming effect.

You can offset the dark colour by painting a light colour above the dado rail and laying a lighter, natural floor covering like sisal or cork tiles. The effect is rich and intense.

This idea can be adapted to any colour scheme you like and you can reverse the effect by using a light background with darker stamps. Experiment with colours and shades and you'll often find that unusual combinations create the most stunning impact.

YOU WILL NEED
emulsion paint in deep blue-green,
sap-green and red
paintbrush
plate
foam roller
large heart stamp
water-based matt varnish and paintbrush
(optional)

1 Paint the wall below the dado rail in deep blue-green. Leave to dry. Spread a small amount of sap-green paint on to the plate and run the roller through it until it is evenly coated. Ink the stamp and begin printing the pattern in groups. Re-ink the stamp only when the print is very light.

2 Gradually build up the pattern all over the wall. The first prints after inking will be solid and bright; the last ones will fade into the background. This is a feature of the design, so make the most of the natural irregularities.

3 This is an optional step. If you find that the contrasts are too strong, mix some varnish with the blue-green paint (one part paint to five parts varnish) and brush it all over the pattern. Leave to dry.

4 Ink the stamp with red paint and over-print every third heart in the top row. Then over-print every third heart in the next row, this time starting one in from the edge. Repeat these two rows to over-print the whole pattern. Re-ink when the colour has faded.

Toy Box

This project gives instant appeal to the most ordinary of wooden boxes. It works just as well on old as new woods but, if you are using an old box, give it a good rub down with medium- and fine-grade sandpaper before you begin. This will remove any sharp edges or splinters.

The lid of the box is given a rust-red background before being stamped with three heart shapes in four colours. The stamps are rotated so that they appear at different angles and the pattern turns out quite randomly. It is best to follow the spirit of the idea rather than adhering rigidly to the instructions. That way, you will end up with a truly individual design.

YOU WILL NEED
hinged wooden chest/box with a lid
(suitable for storing toys)
rust-red emulsion paint
emulsion or acrylic paint in maroon, sap-green, bright green and dark blue
paintbrush
plate
foam roller
small, large and trellis heart stamps
fine-grade sandpaper
matt varnish and paintbrush

1 Paint the box with rust-red paint, applying two coats to give a good matt background. Leave the paint to dry between coats.

2 Spread some maroon paint on to the plate and run the roller through it until it is evenly coated. Use the roller to apply a border round the edge of the lid. Leave to dry.

3 Spread some sap-green paint on to the plate and coat the roller. Ink the small stamp and print a few hearts randomly over the lid of the box.

4 Ink the large and the trellis stamps with the sap-green paint. Print some hearts close together and others on their own to create a random pattern. Cover the whole lid in this way.

5 Clean all three stamps and ink with the bright green paint. Build up the pattern by adding this colour in the gaps, leaving enough space for the last two colours.

6 Using the dark blue paint, continue stamping the three hearts over the lid.

7 Finally, fill in the remaining background space with the maroon paint and the three heart stamps. No large spaces should remain. Leave to dry completely.

8 Use fine-grade sandpaper to rub down the lid where you think natural wear and tear would be the most likely to occur.

9 You can preserve the comfortable "weathered" look of the toy box by applying two coats of matt varnish.

Hallways

Your hallway and reception are the way in which you present your home to the rest of the world and they deserve plenty of thought and care for this reason — after all, the rooms in which you receive your guests will undoubtedly have an effect on their opinion of you! Stamping has to be the easiest way to put a pattern on a wall and to make an impact in just one weekend. Once you have mastered the basic techniques you will begin to develop your own unique style — without any need for great artistic talent. Build your designs around a theme and you are sure to make a lasting impression.

TERRACOTTA ENTRANCE HALL

Corridors, entrance halls and landings are good for "sudden inspiration" decorating jobs, as there is very little furniture to be moved. Make the most of these spaces using warm colours and all-over patterns. The woodwork, table and chair are all painted a pale duck-egg blue, which is also used to stamp the leaf pattern on the semi-transparent blind. You can use fabric paint on the blind but it is not absolutely essential, as the blind is unlikely to be washed. A painted border in the same colour as the tulips adds a very smart finishing touch to the walls and small decorative objects such as the wall sconce can be stamped in similar shades.

YOU WILL NEED
emulsion paint in terracotta, deep plum
and grey-green
large and small paintbrushes
plumbline
25 x 25cm/10 x 10in card
pencil
plates
foam rollers
tulip and leaf stamps
ruler
masking tape (optional)
scrap paper
black stamp pad
scissors
white, semi-transparent roller blind
newspaper
duck-egg blue emulsion paint or
fabric paint
iron (optional)
punched tin wall sconce
fine artist's paintbrush

1 Paint the walls terracotta and leave to dry. Attach the plumbline at ceiling height. Hold the card square against the wall so that the string cuts through the top and bottom corners of the square. Mark all four points in pencil. Continue moving the square and marking the points to form a grid.

2 Spread some deep plum emulsion paint on to a plate and run a roller through it until it is evenly coated. Ink the tulip stamp and, holding it on the diagonal, make a print on each pencil mark. Position the stamp just above or just below the mark each time to create a regular pattern.

3 Change the angle of the stamp from right to left with each alternate print to give the pattern a hand-printed rather than a machine-printed look. Continue stamping tulips until the whole wall is covered.

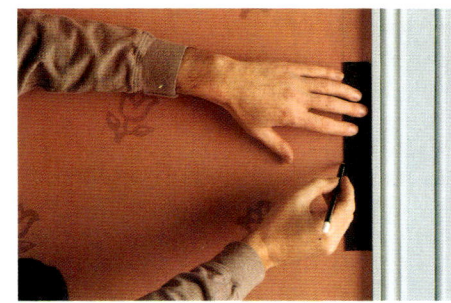

4 Draw a line around the window a ruler's width away from the edge of the window frame. Stick masking tape along the line if you are not confident about painting a straight line.

5 Using a small paintbrush, paint a deep plum border between the edge of the window frame and the pencil line.

6 For the blind, use the stamp pad to print 16 leaves on scrap paper. Cut them out. Lay the blind on newspaper and arrange the leaves to plan the design, starting at the bottom edge.

7 Spread some duck-egg blue emulsion or fabric paint on to a plate and run the roller through it until it is evenly coated. Ink the stamp and remove one paper shape at a time to stamp a leaf in its place.

8 As you complete each row, move the paper patterns up to make the next row, keeping the spacing consistent.

9 Continue in this way until the whole blind is covered. If you are using fabric paint, follow the manufacturer's instructions to seal the paint with an iron.

10 For the wall sconce, spread some deep plum emulsion paint on to a plate and run the roller through it until it is evenly coated. Ink the tulip stamp and stamp one print on the back panel of the sconce.

11 Use a fine artist's paintbrush to paint a grey-green line around the back panel and a thick stripe across the front.

STRIPY HALLWAY

All too often, creative decorating is restricted to the larger rooms of a house, but the hall is the first thing everybody sees when they come through the front door. Why not use stamping to make a stunning first impression on your visitors?

The colour scheme combines two earth colours with bright silver stars to give a slightly Moroccan feel. If you have an immovable carpet or tiles that don't suit these shades, then choose a colour from your existing floor covering to highlight the walls. Hallways seldom have windows to give natural light and the inclination is to use light, bright colours to prevent them from looking gloomy. A better idea is to go for intense, dramatic colours with good electric lighting – they will turn a corridor into a welcoming hallway.

YOU WILL NEED
household sponge
emulsion paint in light coffee and
spicy brown
pencil
plumbline
re-usable adhesive
straight-edged card or wooden plank, the
width required for the stamps
paintbrush
scissors
silver acrylic paint
plate
foam roller
starburst stamp

1 Use a household sponge to apply irregular patches of light coffee emulsion to the wall. Leave to dry.

2 Attach a plumbline at ceiling height with re-usable adhesive so it hangs just away from the wall. Line up one straight edge of the card or plank and use as a guide to draw a straight line in pencil down the wall.

3 Move the card marker one width space along the wall, and continue to mark evenly spaced lines.

4 Paint the first stripe spicy brown. Try to keep within the pencil lines, but don't worry too much about slight mistakes as the wall should look hand-painted and not have the total regularity of wallpaper.

5 Continue painting each alternate stripe, keeping within the pencil lines, but attempting to create a slightly irregular finish.

6 Cut the card spacer to the length required to use as a positional guide for the stars. Spread some silver paint on to the plate and run the roller through it until it is evenly coated. Ink the stamp and print a star in each of

the spicy brown stripes along the wall, above and below the card spacer. Continue printing across the wall, then return to the first stripe and start printing again, one space below the lowest star.

7 Using the card spacer as before, print the first two rows of stars in the coffee-coloured stripes. Position these stars so they fall mid-way between the stars in the spicy brown stripe.

8 Continue this process to fill in the remaining stars all down the coffee-coloured stripes.

TUSCAN HALLWAY

All three stamps are used in this project to transform a dull space into a wall frieze that you will want to preserve forever. The finished wall will bring a touch of Tuscany into your home, even when the sky is a gloomy grey outside. The wall is divided at dado height with a strong burgundy red below and a warm cream above to visually lower the ceiling. The vine leaf pattern has been stamped on to a grid of pencil marks that is simple to measure out using a square of card and a plumbline. The lines are hand-painted using a wooden batten as a hand rest but you could also stick parallel strips of masking tape around the walls and fill in the stripes between.

YOU WILL NEED
tape measure
pencil
ruler
emulsion paint in cream, burgundy,
terracotta, white and black
large household paintbrush
wallpaper paste, mixed according to the
manufacturer's instructions
plate
foam roller
grape, leaf and tendril stamps
thin strip of card
long-bristled lining brush
straight-edged wooden batten, 1m/1yd
long
plumbline
15 x 15cm/6 x 6in card
square-tipped artist's paintbrush
clear gloss, matt or satin varnish
and brush

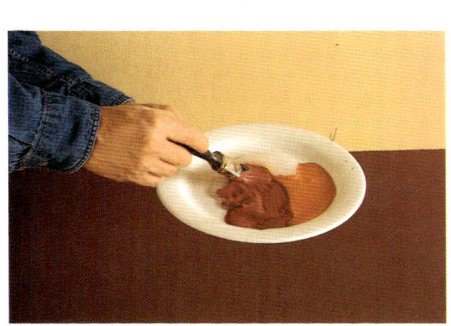

1 Measure the height of a dado rail and draw a line around the wall with a ruler and pencil. Paint the wall above the line cream and the area below burgundy. Mix roughly equal amounts of wallpaper paste, burgundy and terracotta paint on a plate.

2 Run the roller through the mixture until it is evenly coated and ink the grape stamp. Align the strip of card with the top of the burgundy section. Rest the base of the stamp block on the card to stamp a row of grapes.

3 Ink the tendril stamp and stamp a tendril at the top of each bunch of grapes. Allow some prints to be paler than others as the paint wears off the stamp block, to give a faded and patchy effect.

4 Mix a little cream paint into some white. With the lining brush, apply highlights to the grapes and the tendrils. Let the brushstrokes vary in direction and weight to add to the hand-painted look. Support your painting hand with your free hand. ▶

5 Hold the batten just below the top edge of the burgundy section and rest your painting hand on it. Slide your hand along the batten to paint a smooth, thin line in off-white. Practise this movement first and try to relax your hand to avoid jerky lines. A slight waviness to the line will not spoil the effect. Try to avoid having to paint over the line, as a single, fresh brushstroke looks better.

6 Attach a plumbline above dado height, just in from one corner and so that it hangs down to the skirting board. Place the card square against the wall so that the string cuts through the top and bottom corners. Mark all the corner points in pencil.

7 Move the card down so that the top corner rests on the lowest pencil mark. Complete one column of the grid in this way, then move the plumbline across and continue until the lower wall is completely covered with a grid of pencil marks.

8 Mix a small amount of black paint into the burgundy to deepen the colour. Spread some dark burgundy paint on to a plate and run the roller through it until it is evenly coated. Ink the leaf stamp and make a print on one of the pencil marks.

9 Position the stamp just above or just below the pencil mark each time to create a regular pattern over the whole lower wall.

10 Move the batten about 2.5cm/ 1in from the cream dado line and use the square-tipped artist's brush to paint a second, broader line. Keep the line as fresh as possible; visible brushstrokes are preferable to solid, flat colour. Apply a coat of varnish to the lower wall to seal and protect the paint.

MEDIEVAL HALLWAY

Decorate your hallway using medieval patterns and colours that will make coming through the front door a pleasure for you and your visitors. Hallways can seem dark and narrow, but this can be dealt with by using two colours of paint. A dark colour above dado height creates the illusion of a lower ceiling, while a light colour below, combined with a light floor covering, seems to push the walls outwards to give the impression of width. The crown pattern is stamped in a diagonal grid, which is easy to draw using a plumbline and a square of card.

YOU WILL NEED
pencil
emulsion paint in dark blue-green,
buttermilk yellow and light cream
paintbrush
fine-grade sandpaper
masking tape
ruler
paint roller
wallpaper paste (mixed following the
manufacturer's instructions)
plate
foam roller
diamond and crown stamps
plumbline
15 x 15cm/6 x 6in card

1 Draw a horizontal pencil line on the wall, at dado height. Paint the top half in blue-green and the bottom in buttermilk yellow. When dry, lightly sand the blue-green paint. Stick a strip of masking tape along the lower edge of the blue-green, and another 10cm/4in below. Apply light cream with a dry roller over the buttermilk yellow.

2 Stick another length of masking tape 2cm/5in below the one marking the edge of the green section. Using a paintbrush and blue-green paint, fill in the stripe between the two lower strips of tape. Leave to dry and peel off the tape. Lightly sand the blue-green stripe to give it the appearance of the upper section of wall.

3 On a plate, mix one part blue-green emulsion with two parts pre-mixed wallpaper paste and stir well. Ink the diamond stamp with the foam roller and stamp a row of diamonds on the narrow cream stripe.

4 Use a plumbline and a card square to mark an all-over grid on the cream half of the wall. This will be used as a guide for the crown stamps.

5 Ink the crown stamp with the blue-green emulsion and wallpaper paste mixture and stamp a motif on each pencil mark. Make several prints before re-inking to create variation in the density of the prints.

GOTHIC CUPBOARD

Visit junk shops to find old pieces of furniture with some interesting detailing and panels that would take a stamped heraldic design. This small bedside cupboard looked very gloomy with its original dark woodstain, but has shed its old image and become a complete extrovert as the centrepiece of the medieval entrance hall.

YOU WILL NEED
small wooden cupboard
fine-grade sandpaper
emulsion paint in rust-brown, dark blue-green, lilac and yellow-ochre
paintbrush
medium-sized artist's paintbrush
black stamp pad
diamond and fleur-de-lys stamps
scrap paper
scissors
pencil
ruler (optional)
plates
foam rollers
red-orange smooth-flowing water-based paint (thinned emulsion, poster paint or ready-mixed watercolour)
lining brush
shellac and brush
water-based tinted varnish
fine wire wool

1 Sand away the existing varnish or paint. Paint the cupboard in rust-brown on the main body and blue-green on any carved details and on the panels. Use the artist's brush to paint the blue-green right into the panel edges, to ensure even coverage.

2 Use the stamp pad to print the diamond and fleur-de-lys motifs on paper and cut them out. Lay them on the panels to plan your pattern. Make a small pencil mark on the panel at the base point of each motif as a guide for stamping. Use a ruler if necessary to make sure the design is symmetrical. Mark the base point of the motif on the back of each stamp block so that you can line up the marks when you print.

3 Spread some lilac paint on to a plate and run the roller through it until it is evenly coated. Ink the diamond stamp and print diamonds using the pencil marks as a guide.

4 Spread some yellow-ochre paint on to a plate and ink the fleur-de-lys stamp. Print the fleur-de-lys designs, using the pencil marks as a guide.

5 Using red-orange paint and the lining brush, add hand-painted details to the motifs. Support your painting hand with your spare hand resting on the surface of the cupboard and aim to get a smooth, flowing line.

6 Apply a coat of shellac to seal the surface for varnishing and leave to dry. Apply a fairly thick coat of tinted varnish and leave to dry. Rub the raised areas and edges of the cupboard with fine wire wool to simulate natural wear and tear.

HEAVENLY HALLWAY

The cherubs are stamped in silhouette on this hallway wall, framed in medallions of pale yellow on a dove-grey background. The yellow medallions are stencilled on to the grey background and the combination of colours softens the potentially hard-edged dark silhouettes. The stencil can be cut from card or transparent mylar and the paint is applied with the same roller that is used for inking the stamps. The cherubic theme is extended to the painted wooden key box and the lampshade.

YOU WILL NEED
emulsion paint in dove-grey, pale yellow
and charcoal-grey
household paintbrushes
plumbline
25 x 25cm/10 x 10in card
pencil
ruler
stencil card
scalpel or craft knife
cutting mat
plates
foam rollers
cherub and swag stamps
lidded wooden box
fine-grade sandpaper
cloth
burnt-umber artist's oil colour
cream fabric lampshade and ceramic
lamp base
black stamp pad
scrap paper
scissors
masking tape

1 Paint the wall dove-grey and leave to dry. Attach a plumbline at ceiling height, just in from one corner. Hold the card square against the wall so that the string cuts through the top and bottom corners. Mark all the corner points in pencil. Move the card and continue marking the wall to make a grid for the stamps.

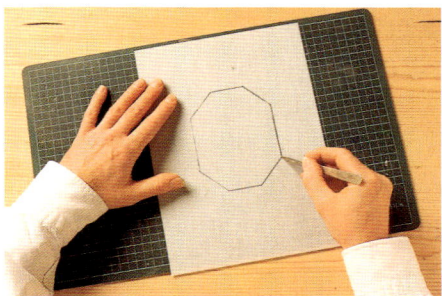

2 Use a pencil and ruler to draw the medallion shape on a sheet of stencil card. Carefully cut out the stencil using a scalpel or craft knife on a cutting mat. Spread yellow emulsion paint on to a plate and run the roller through it until it is evenly coated.

3 Position the stencil on one of the pencil marks and use the paint-covered roller to stencil the medallion shape. Paint all the medallions in this way, positioning the stencil in the same place on each pencil mark.

4 Ink the first cherub stamp with charcoal-grey paint and make a print inside each medallion.

5 Paint the wooden box pale yellow, inside and out, and leave to dry.

6 Spread some charcoal-grey paint on to a plate and run a roller through it until it is evenly coated. Ink the second cherub stamp and make a print in the centre of the box lid. Print the swag stamp directly beneath the cherub.

7 Measure the sides of the box to determine the number of swag prints that will fit comfortably in a row. Mark the positions in pencil or judge by eye to add swags around the sides of the box. Leave to dry.

8 Rub the corners and edges of the box with fine-grade sandpaper. Rub the prints in places to add a faded, aged look. Use a cloth to rub burnt-umber artist's oil colour on to the whole box, to give an antique appearance.

9 For the lampshade, stamp several swags on scrap paper and cut them out. Arrange the cut-outs on the lampshade to plan your design. Hold each piece in place with a small piece of masking tape.

10 Spread some dove-grey paint on to a plate and run a roller through it until it is evenly coated. Ink the swag stamp and print swags around the top of the lampshade, removing each paper motif before you stamp in its place.

11 Continue stamping around the base of the shade in the same way, removing each paper motif in turn.

12 Stamp swags around the lamp base to complete the co-ordinated look. Judge the positioning by eye or use paper motifs as before.

ROSE HALLWAY

New homes are wonderfully fresh, but the perfectly-even walls can look plain if you are used to details such as dado-rails and deep skirting boards. This project shows you how to retain the freshness of new pastel paintwork and add interest with a frieze at dado-rail height and a coat of colourwash below it.

Don't worry about painting in a straight line for the frieze – just use two strips of low-tack masking tape and paint between them. You could even try doing it by hand, as it does add character to the decoration, even if you do wobble a bit!

Wooden furniture is given a distressed paint finish in toning colours, and stamped with the rose designs to co-ordinate with the walls.

YOU WILL NEED
sandpaper (optional)
emulsion paint in cream, blue-green, dusky-blue and peach
paintbrush
cloth
plates
foam roller
scrap paper
rosebud, small rose and large rose stamps
tape measure
pencil
wallpaper paste (made up according to the manufacturer's instructions)
masking tape
spirit level
straight-edged plank of wood
square-tipped 2.5cm/1in artist's brush

2 Spread the dusky-blue paint on to the plate and run the roller through it. Ink the rosebud stamp and print the design on to the paper.

3 Referring to the paper pattern, stamp the design in position on your chosen piece of furniture.

1 To prepare the furniture, rub each piece down with sandpaper and apply a coat of cream paint. Make the blue-green glaze by diluting one part paint with three parts water and then brush it on following the direction of the grain. Before the paint has dried, use a cloth to wipe off some of the paint.

4 Stamp more rosebuds on either side of the central design. Work with the shape of the furniture to decide upon the best position and the number of prints.

5 If you are decorating a desk or dresser, unscrew and remove any handles, then stamp the pattern on the drawer fronts. Screw them back after the paint has dried.

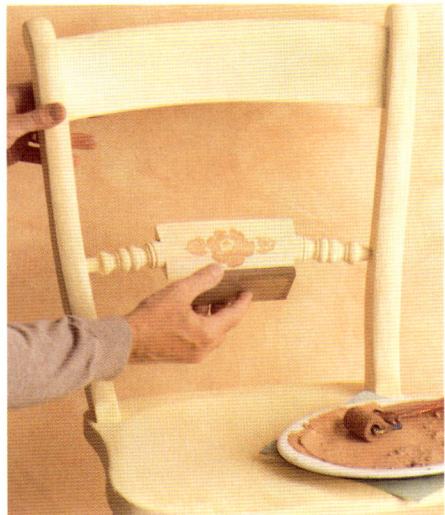

6 For a small piece of furniture like this chair, a simple design is best. Paint the chair cream, then print a single small rose in peach.

7 To make the colourwash for the walls, mix one part peach emulsion paint with one part wallpaper paste and four parts water. Make it up in multiples of six. It is best to make more than you need, so that you can do the whole room from the same batch to ensure a colour match.

Unless the room has been painted recently, apply a coat of cream emulsion to the walls.

8 Measure about 90cm/36in from the floor and make a pencil mark on the wall. Tape the spirit level to the plank and draw a straight line all round the room 90cm/36in above floor level. Draw another line 3cm/1¼in above it.

9 Apply the colourwash below the line using sweeping random brushstrokes. If runs occur, just pick them up with the brush and work them into the surrounding wall. Aim for a patchy, mottled effect.

10 If you have a steady hand, paint the dusky-blue stripe with the square-tipped brush, otherwise use masking tape to guide you and remove it when dry.

11 Spread the dusky-blue and peach paints on to the plates and use the foam roller or paintbrush to ink the large rose stamp, using the colours as shown. Print with the stamp base resting on the top of the blue stripe. Continue all round the room, re-inking each time for a regular print.

TUMBLING ROSE CHAIR COVER

Ready-made slip covers for director's and wicker chairs provide an innovative way of restyling a room. It is rather like putting on a new jacket and changing your image.

The design of the roses follows the curve of the chair and the direction of the seat. One of the advantages of these covers, is that you can use them to disguise less than perfect chairs that are still structurally sound. Look out for old Lloyd loom chairs with sprung seats – their appearance may have been spoiled by coats of gloss paint over the years, but they're still ideal for a slip cover.

YOU WILL NEED
fabric paint in green and red
plate
foam rollers
large rose stamp
ready-made calico slip cover
backing paper (such as thin card or newspaper)
iron

1 Spread some green and red paint on to the plate and run the rollers through them until they are evenly coated. Ink the rose red and the stalk and leaves green.

2 Place the backing paper behind the front panel of the slip cover and begin stamping the roses. Rotate the stamp in your hand after each print to get the tumbling rose effect.

3 Place the backing paper behind the seat section and stamp the roses in the same way as the front.

4 Place the backing sheet inside the top section and stamp the top row, following the shape of the slip cover. Continue stamping to fill the cover, rotating the stamp as you did before. Fix the fabric paint on the chair cover with a hot iron following the manufacturer's instructions.

DETAILS & ACCESSORIES

THE ABILITY TO ACCESSORIZE AND PAY ATTENTION TO FINE DETAIL IS A

VALUABLE ASSET WHICH WILL ADD VISUAL INTEREST TO ANY ROOM AND

GIVES SUBSTANTIAL WEIGHT TO ANY THEME YOU MAY CHOOSE TO ADOPT.

THESE FINAL TOUCHES MAKE YOUR INTERIORS PARTICULAR TO YOU. THEY ARE

ALSO THE IDEAL STARTING POINT IF YOU ARE NEW TO THE IDEA OF

STAMP DECORATING. EXPERIMENT WITH COLOURS AND STAMP DESIGNS ON

SHEETS OF PLAIN GIFTWRAP AND YOU WILL BE AMAZED AT HOW

GOOD THE PAPER WILL LOOK WITH EVEN THE MOST BASIC OF STAMP ARRANGEMENTS.

SEE HOW EFFECTIVE A SIMPLE, STRONG MOTIF CAN BE AND THEN START ADDING

OTHER MORE COMPLICATED DESIGNS TO YOUR COLLECTION.

CHERUB SHOPPING BAG

Large canvas shopping bags with shoulder straps are both fashionable and useful. They come in a range of plain colours that seem to cry out to be given an individual touch. Stamping works well on canvas and you can choose from fabric paint, acrylics or household emulsion. Bear in mind that you will not be able to wash the bag if you use emulsion or acrylic, while fabric paint can be fixed with an iron to make it permanent and washable.

YOU WILL NEED
blue canvas shopping bag
backing card
cherub and swag stamps
black stamp pad
scrap paper
scissors
emulsion, acrylic or fabric paint in white
and pale blue
plate
foam roller
iron (optional)

1 Lay the bag on a flat surface and insert the backing card to prevent the paint from passing through to the other side.

2 Make several cherub and swag prints on scrap paper. Cut them out and arrange them on the bag to plan your design.

3 Spread some white paint on to the plate and run the roller through it until it is evenly coated. Ink the cherub and swag stamps and print the pattern, removing each paper motif and stamping in its place. Leave to dry, then ink the edges of the stamps with pale blue paint. Over-print the white design to create a shadow effect. If using fabric paint, follow the paint manufacturer's instructions to fix the design with an iron.

CUPID MUGS

Considering the range of mugs produced, it can be extraordinarily difficult to find one that has the shape, colour and pattern that you like. This project mixes and matches the colours of the mugs and patterns, while sticking to the same simple shape. Mugs can be successfully stamped with acrylic enamel paints and "fired" in a domestic oven to make the design permanent. Follow the manufacturer's instructions and the paint will then withstand the hottest washing-up water.

YOU WILL NEED
four mugs in different colours
acrylic enamel paints in the same four
colours (or as close as possible)
four plates
foam roller
cherub stamps

1 Wash the mugs in hot water and detergent and dry thoroughly. Spread one colour of acrylic enamel paint on to each of the plates. Decide which colour to stamp on each mug.

2 Run the roller through one of the colours until it is evenly coated and use it to ink the stamp. Stamp the cherub on the first mug, removing the stamp directly to prevent it from sliding on the smooth surface.

3 Wash and dry the roller and stamp, then re-ink and stamp the second mug. Stamp all four mugs in this way, using both cherub stamps. Follow the manufacturer's instructions to "fire" the mugs in a domestic oven to make the design permanent.

VINTAGE GLASS BOWL

Turn a plain glass bowl into an exquisite table centrepiece by stamping a white tendril pattern on the outside. Stamped glassware looks wonderful because the opaque patterns seem to intermingle as you look through the transparent glass. Another advantage is that you can see the stamp as the print is being made, which helps you to position it correctly and avoid overlaps and smudges. Glass painting has become popular recently and there are several brands of specialist glass paint available. Acrylic enamel paint has a good consistency for stamping and is water-based, allowing you to simply wipe it off and start again if you make a mistake.

YOU WILL NEED
plain glass bowl
clean cloth
white acrylic enamel paint
plate
foam roller
tendril stamp

1 Wash the bowl in hot water and detergent, then wipe dry to ensure that there is no grease on the surface. Spread some white acrylic enamel paint on to a plate and run the roller through it until it is evenly coated.

2 Ink the tendril stamp and stamp the first row of prints around the base of the bowl. Remove the stamp directly, taking care that it does not slide or smudge the print. If you do make a mistake, wipe off the paint with a clean cloth and start again.

3 Turn the stamp the other way up to stamp the second row, positioning the prints in between the tendrils on the first row, so that there are no obvious gaps.

4 Stamp one more row with the stamp the original way up. Allow the stamp to overlap the edge of the bowl, so that most of the stem is left out. Leave the bowl to dry or "fire" it in the oven to fix the design, following the paint manufacturer's instructions.

PINEAPPLE PLACE MATS

Place mats seem to cost a disproportionate amount of money and the designs available are very limited. These mats are cut from MDF and painted a deep rich blue before being stamped and outlined in light blue. This classic colour combination would suit a formal dinner setting, while using brighter colours will give a tropical look. Experiment with colours and decorate a set of mats to suit your own style of entertaining.

YOU WILL NEED
medium artist's paintbrush or lining brush
light blue emulsion paint
mats cut from thin MDF,
painted dark blue
plate
foam roller
pineapple stamp
clear satin varnish and brush

1 Using a medium artist's paintbrush or lining brush and light blue emulsion, paint a line around the edge of each mat. Support your painting hand with your free hand as you work.

2 Spread some light blue paint on to a plate and run the roller through it until it is evenly coated. Ink the pineapple stamp and stamp a single print in the centre of the mat.

3 Stamp an angled print on either side of the first. Seal and protect the mat with several coats of clear satin varnish, allowing each coat to dry before applying the next.

TABLE NAPKINS

These stamped table napkins look great with rush mats on a wooden table top. They bring together even the most casual collection of plates, glasses and cutlery to look like a deliberate choice. You can buy a set of plain table napkins or make your own by sewing straight seams along the edges of squares of cotton fabric. Stamping on fabric is easy and special fabric paints can be heat-treated with a hot iron to make the pattern permanent. Follow the manufacturer's instructions, which may vary from brand to brand.

YOU WILL NEED
terracotta-coloured table napkins
iron
newspaper
cream-coloured fabric paint
plate
foam roller
grape and tendril stamps

2 Stamp a bunch of grapes halfway along each edge, then ink the tendril stamp and print tendrils between the grapes. Stamp all the napkins in this way and leave to dry. Seal the design with an iron, following the paint manufacturer's instructions.

1 Wash and iron the napkins to remove any glaze which may block the paint's absorption. Lay the first napkin on top of several sheets of newspaper. Spread some cream fabric paint on to a plate and run the roller through it until it is evenly coated. Ink the grape stamp and print a bunch of grapes in each corner of the napkin.

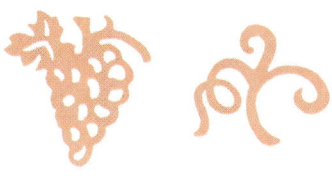

PICTURE FRAME

This project combines all the creative possibilities of stamping. It involves four processes: painting a background, stamping in one colour, over-printing in a second colour and rubbing back to the wood. These processes transform a plain wooden frame and they are neither time consuming nor expensive.

It is surprisingly difficult to find small, old frames that are broad enough to stamp. Fortunately, a wide range of basic, cheap frames can be found in DIY stores.

YOU WILL NEED
picture frame
emulsion paint in sky-blue, red-brown
and gold
paintbrush
plate
foam roller
small and large star stamp
fine wire wool or sandpaper

1 Paint the frame sky-blue and leave it to dry thoroughly.

2 Spread a small amount of red-brown paint on to the plate and run the roller through it until it is evenly coated. Ink the first stamp and print it in the middle of each side.

3 Using the red-brown paint, stamp a large star over each corner. Leave to dry thoroughly.

4 Ink the large stamp with gold and over-print the red-brown corner stars. Let dry before rubbing the frame gently with steel wool or sandpaper. Experiment with dropped shadow effects and other designs.

GOTHIC DISPLAY PLATE

Large china display plates look great on the wall and they don't have to be confined to country kitchen-type interiors, as demonstrated by this bold pattern. The plate used here is a large platter with a pale blue border outlined in navy, although the design can also be stamped on a plain plate. Use acrylic enamel paint on ceramics and glassware. It can be baked in a household oven following the manufacturer's instructions. The resulting patterns are very hard-wearing and even seem to stand up to dishwashers and scouring pads, but the paints are recommended for display rather than food use.

YOU WILL NEED
black stamp pad
diamond and crown stamps
scrap paper
scissors
display plate
acrylic enamel paint in navy blue and deep orange
plates
foam rollers
ruler

1 Use the stamp pad to print eight diamond motifs and one crown on paper and cut them out. Arrange them on the plate to design the border pattern and central motif.

2 Spread some navy blue acrylic enamel paint on to a plate and run the roller through it until it is evenly coated. Ink the diamond stamp, then remove one of the paper shapes and stamp a diamond in its place.

3 Place a ruler under the plate, so that it runs centrally from the printed motif to the one opposite. Line up the stamp with the edge of the ruler to print the second motif. Print the motifs on the other two sides in the same way, then fill in the diamonds in between, judging by eye.

4 Ink the crown stamp with deep orange paint and stamp a single crown in the centre of the plate. Bake the plate in the oven, following the manufacturer's instructions.

WEDDING ALBUM COVER

Custom-made wedding photograph albums are never as special as one you make yourself. For most of us, a wedding is the only time we are photographed professionally looking our very best, so the presentation should do the pictures justice. The album should have a solid spine, so don't choose the spiral-bound type. Visit a specialist paper dealer and discover the wonderful range of textured papers. The paper is stamped with gold size and gold leaf is laid on to it to create gleaming golden cherubs and swags. Initials or the date of the wedding add the finishing touch.

YOU WILL NEED
white textured paper
large photograph album with a solid spine
scissors or scalpel
double-sided sticky tape
cherub and swag stamps
black stamp pad
scrap paper
gold size
plate
foam roller
gold transfer leaf
soft-bristled paintbrush
gold transfer letters or fine artist's brush

1 Lay the opened album on the sheet of paper and trim the paper to size. Allow a border round the edges to fold over the paper inside the cover. Cover the album with the paper, sticking down the overlaps on the inside of the cover.

2 Stamp several cherubs and swags on scrap paper and cut them out. Lay them out on the album cover with any initials or dates to plan your design. When you are happy with the design, use the paper cut-outs as a guide for positioning the stamps.

3 Spread some gold size on to a plate and run the roller through it until it is evenly coated. Ink the stamps with size and stamp the design on the album cover. Leave to dry for the time recommended by the manufacturer until the size becomes tacky.

4 Lay sheets of gold leaf on to the size and burnish with a soft brush.

5 Brush away any excess gold leaf still clinging to the paper. Add initials and the date, if required, using gold transfer letters or paint them freehand in size and gild as before.

BOOK COVERS AND SECRETS BOX

This project evokes another era, when time passed by more slowly and leisure had nothing to do with aerobic exercise. Diaries and scrapbooks were kept and lovingly covered with printed papers and secret mementoes were hidden in locked wooden caskets. Recapture the spirit of a bygone age by stamping patterned papers and using them to bind sketch books, albums and diaries. Preserve the battered antiquity of an old wooden box by stamping it and lining it in muted shades of red and green, then rubbing back the paint to simulate years of wear and tear.

YOU WILL NEED
black stamp pad
tulip, leaf and pineapple stamps
scrap paper
sugar paper
ready-mixed watercolour paint in a droppered bottle in deep red, leaf-green and black
plates
long ruler
diary, photo album, or book, such as a sketch book
PVA glue
black bookbinding tape
cutting mat
scalpel or craft knife
old wooden box
emulsion or acrylic paint in brick-red and sage-green
foam roller
5 x 2.5cm/2 x 1in wooden batten
lining brush
fine sandpaper or wire wool
furniture polish (optional)

1 For the book cover, use the stamp pad and print four tulips on scrap paper. Cut them out and arrange them in a row along the top edge of the sugar paper, side by side and alternately facing up and down. Use these paper prints as a guide for stamping.

2 Spread some deep red watercolour paint on to a plate and dip the stamp into it. Lay the ruler across the paper and use to align the stamp to print the first row. Re-ink the stamp after three prints to give an irregular hand-printed effect.

3 Move the ruler down the width of a stamp block for each new row. Stamp the rows so that the tulips lie between the prints in the previous row. Cover the paper completely and leave to dry. Print more paper, using the leaf and pineapple stamps and the leaf-green and black paint.

4 Cover the book with the paper, sticking down any mitred corners with PVA glue. Stick a strip of bookbinding tape along the spine to cover the paper edges and so there is an equal width of tape on the front and back cover. Trim away the tape at the top and bottom with a scalpel.

5 For the secrets box, use the stamp pad to print some tulips and leaves on scrap paper and cut them out. Arrange them on the wooden box to plan your design, deciding which motifs will be red and which green.

6 Spread some brick-red emulsion or acrylic paint on to a plate and run the roller through it until it is evenly coated. Ink the stamps and remove one paper shape at a time to stamp a leaf or tulip motif in its place.

7 Ink the leaf stamp with sage-green paint and stamp green leaves on the box in the same way.

8 Place the batten along the edge of the box and use the sage-green paint and the lining brush to paint an outline around the box and corner motifs. Slide your hand along the batten to keep an even line.

9 Leave the paint to dry completely, then lightly distress the stamped prints with sandpaper or wire wool. The box can then be polished with furniture polish, if desired.

SEAHORSE THROW

Throws are indispensable accessories in every home – while adding glorious
swatches of colours to any room, they also cleverly disguise any worn or stained patches.
Throws can be thick and wintry or light and airy like this one, which could also double up as a
sarong for a quick wrap-around. Crêped cotton has a fine, crinkled texture, which adds volume to
the fabric and makes it drape well. Cotton or other natural fibres are the best choice as they absorb
the fabric paint easily. So, have a go at this throw and make a luxurious gold design
for your home.

YOU WILL NEED

*length of crêped cotton or a ready-made
plain throw
backing paper (such as thin card or
newspaper)
drawing pins
gold fabric paint
plate
foam roller
seahorse and shell stamps
iron*

1 Protect your work surface with backing paper. Lay the fabric over this and pin down.

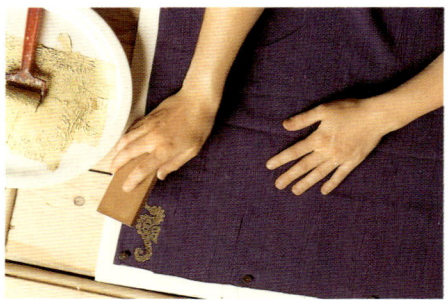

2 Spread some gold fabric paint onto the plate and run the roller through it until it is evenly coated. Ink the seahorse stamp and make the first print in one corner.

3 Print a border along the top and bottom edges of the throw, alternating shells and seahorses.

4 Stamp widely spaced rows of seahorses between the borders, turning the stamp 180° each print. The prints in each row should fall between those of the previous row. Fix the fabric paint with a hot iron following the manufacturer's instructions. Press directly down on to the fabric, ensuring the fabric retains its texture.

CHRISTENING PARTY

The gift paper, cards and table setting of this project will all help to make a traditional christening or naming day party an unforgettable occasion. Use the cherubs to announce the baby's birth and then herald the start of the celebrations. Buy a good-quality white paper for the cards. Some papers are deckle-edged, while others are textured. The choice is a personal one and a textured surface will give interesting stamped effects, so experiment on samples of paper. Set off the hand-printed wrapping paper with white satin ribbons and bows.

YOU WILL NEED
large white tablecloth or sheet
backing card
fabric paint in bottle-green and silver
plates
foam rollers
swag and cherub stamps
iron
paper napkins in white and bottle-green
acrylic paint in bottle-green, white and blue-grey
white note-paper
scissors
ruler
pencil
water-based size
silver transfer leaf
fine wire wool
silver wrapping paper
newspaper
black stamp pad
scrap paper
small strip of card

1 Lay the tablecloth or sheet on a table. Ink the swag stamp with bottle-green fabric paint and print across one corner of the cloth, so that the tassels are about 2.5cm/1in from the edges. Stamp swags all around the edge of the cloth to create a scalloped effect.

2 Spread some silver fabric paint on to a plate and run a roller through it until it is evenly coated. Ink both cherub stamps and, alternating the two designs, make a print above every other swag.

3 Continue to stamp a widely spaced cherub pattern in the centre of the cloth, alternating both stamps and rotating the direction of the prints. Follow the manufacturer's instructions to fix the paint with an iron.

4 For the napkins, spread some green acrylic paint on to a plate and run a roller through it until it is evenly coated. Ink the cherub stamps and make one print on each white table napkin.

5 Spread some white acrylic paint on to a plate. Use a roller to ink the cherub stamps. Stamp a white cherub on each green napkin.

6 To make the cards, cut and fold the paper to the required size, which should be at least 14 x 11.5cm/5½ x 4½in. Draw pencil lines on the back of the stamp block to mark the mid-points on each side to help you position the stamp accurately each time. Spread some blue-grey acrylic paint on to a plate and run a roller through it until it is evenly coated. Ink the stamp and print cherubs on all the cards. Leave to dry.

7 Spread water-based size on to a plate and run a roller through it until it is evenly coated. Ink the cherub stamps with size and overprint the blue-grey prints. Leave to dry for the time recommended by the manufacturer until the size becomes tacky. Lay sheets of silver leaf on to the size and burnish the backing paper with a soft cloth.

8 Remove the backing paper and use wire wool to rub away any excess silver leaf still clinging to the paper.

9 To make the wrapping paper, lay the silver paper on some newspaper on a flat surface. Stamp several cherubs and swags on scrap paper and cut them out. Arrange the paper motifs on the silver paper to plan your design. Cut a card strip as a guide to the spacing between the motifs.

10 Spread some bottle-green acrylic paint on to a plate and run a roller through it until it is evenly coated. Ink the cherub stamp and print cherubs on the silver paper. Use the card strip to space the stamps.

11 Ink the swag stamp with white paint and print the linking swags between the cherubs.

WRAPPING PAPER

Imagine never having to buy a sheet of wrapping paper again. Once you realize how easy it is to make stamped paper, there will be no turning back. Stamped paper not only looks great, but it costs so little that you will have lots of spare cash to spend on ribbon and trimmings.

Any plain paper can be stamped. The contrast between utilitarian brown parcel wrap and luxurious gold stars looks particularly striking, but for a more colourful paper, you could use tissue paper, which is available in a riotous assortment of colours.

Only the most exclusive and expensive types of commercial wrapping paper are hand-printed, so you can have the pleasure of stamping your own at a fraction of the cost.

YOU WILL NEED
ruler
pencil
brown parcel wrap
acrylic paint in brown, blue, white
and cream
plate
foam roller
starburst, folk-art and
small star stamps

1 Use the ruler and pencil to mark one edge of the parcel wrap at approximately 12cm/5in intervals.

2 Spread a small amount of brown paint on to the plate and run the roller through it until it is evenly coated. Ink the starburst stamp and print on to the parcel wrap, using the pencil marks as a guide for the first row and judging the next rows visually.

3 Ink the folk-art stamp with blue paint and stamp these stars between the brown stars.

4 Ink the small star stamp with white paint and fill in the centres of the blue stars.

5 Stamp cream stars along diagonal lines between the blue stars.

ANGEL T-SHIRTS

Fabric paints are very easy to use, come in a wide range of colours and can be fixed with a hot iron to make them washable and permanent. The cherubs can be used in many ways, including the funky colour combinations chosen here. Strong contrasts, complimentary shades or dayglo colours will all give the cherub a new image. By overprinting the cherubs slightly off-register in a second colour, you can add a three-dimensional look, too. Wash and iron the T-shirt before printing to remove any glazes that may block the absorption of the fabric paint.

YOU WILL NEED
plain-coloured T-shirts
backing card
cherub and swag stamps
black stamp pad
scrap paper
scissors
fabric paint in various colours
plate
foam roller
ruler (optional)
iron

1 Lay a T-shirt on a flat surface and insert the backing card to prevent the paint from passing through to the other side.

2 Stamp several cherubs or cherubs and swags on scrap paper. Cut them out and arrange them on the T-shirt to plan your design.

3 Spread some fabric paint on to a plate and run the roller through it until it is evenly coated. Ink the cherub stamp and print the pattern, removing each paper motif and stamping a cherub in its place. Re-ink the stamp after each print and press down firmly with the stamp to allow the fabric paint to penetrate the fabric.

4 Use a ruler to help align the pattern if necessary. Experiment with other patterns and colours. Follow the paint manufacturer's instructions to fix the design with an iron.

HERALDIC STATIONERY

Design and print an exclusive set of stationery to add a touch of class to all your correspondence. Heraldic motifs have been used for centuries to decorate letters and secret diaries, but it is no longer necessary to live in a palace to be able to use them. This project demonstrates the variety of ways in which a single stamp can be used to produce different effects. The resulting stationery is all on a theme but with plenty of individual flourishes. Experiment with your favourite colour combinations and try all-over or border patterns to add even more variety. Stamp specialists sell special embossing powders that can be heated to produce a raised print.

YOU WILL NEED
dark blue artist's watercolour
plate
foam rollers
diamond, fleur-de-lys and crown stamps
brown parcel wrap
scalpel or craft knife
cutting mat
small notebook, folder, postcards and
textured and plain notepaper
gold paint
dark blue paper
ruler
set square
paper glue
fine artist's brush

1 Spread some dark blue artist's watercolour on to a plate and run the roller through it until it is evenly coated. Ink the diamond stamp and print one motif on to a small piece of brown parcel wrap.

2 Cut out the diamond shape with a scalpel or craft knife on a cutting mat. Try not to overcut the corners because the shape will be used as a stencil and the paint may bleed through.

3 Position the paper stencil in the middle of the notebook cover and use the roller to apply blue watercolour through it. Leave to dry.

4 Spread some gold paint on to a plate and run the roller through it until it is evenly coated. Ink the diamond stamp and stamp a gold print directly over the solid blue diamond, lining up the edges as closely as possible.

5 Cut a rectangle the size of the fleur-de-lys stamp block out of dark blue paper. Measure to divide it in half lengthways. Cut away one side, with a scalpel or a craft knife, leaving a narrow border around the edge to make a window in one side.

6 Using a ruler and set square to position the stamp, print a dark blue fleur-de-lys in the centre of the folder. Glue the blue paper over the print so that half the fleur-de-lys shows through the window.

7 Ink the fleur-de-lys stamp with gold paint. Cover the cut-out side of the design with a straight-edged piece of parcel wrap. Stamp a gold fleur-de-lys to align with the sides of the blue print. Remove the piece of parcel wrap to reveal the final design, which is half gold and half blue.

8 Stamp a blue fleur-de-lys on a notebook cover or postcard. Cover one half of it with a straight-edged piece of parcel wrap and over-print in gold to make a two-colour print.

9 Fold a piece of textured notepaper
to make a card. Stamp a blue fleur-de-
lys on the front of the card. The
texture will show through in places.
Add flourishes of gold paint using a
fine artist's brush.

10 Stamp a gold crown at the top
of plain white sheets of notepaper.

SUPPLIERS

The following companies supply a wide range of stamps. If you are not able to find
the designs you like, it is sometimes possible to have them made up.

UNITED KINGDOM
Blade Rubber Stamp Company
2 Neal's Yard
London WC2H 9DP
tel: 0171 379 7391

Blue Cat Toy Company
Builders Yard
Silver Street
South Cerney
Gloucestershire GL7 4TS
tel: 01285 851 867
fax: 01285 862 153

First Class Stamps Ltd
The Maltings
Hall Staithe
Fakenham
Norfolk NR21 9BW
tel: 01328 851 449
fax: 01328 864 828

The Stamp Connection
14 Edith Road
Faversham
Kent ME13 8SD
tel/fax: 01795 531 860

Rubber Stampede
c/o Crafty Ideas
6 The Arcade
Hitchen
Hertfordshire
tel: 01462 434 250
fax: 01234 342 156

AUSTRALIA
Annaleey Crafts
PO Box 66
Yeelanna SA 5632
tel: 086 765 026
fax: 086 765 014

Artarama Stamps
39 Landsdowne Parade
Oatley NSW 2223
tel: 02 580 8295
fax: 02 580 5172

Inky Pinky
21 Church Street
Hawthorn Vic 3122
tel: 03 9853 3055
fax: 03 9853 0135

Krafty Lady
No 9 Edgewood Road
Dandenong Vic 3175
tel/fax: 03 9794 6064

Print Blocks Pty Ltd
441 Waterworks Road, Ashgrove
Brisbane Qld 4060
tel: 07 3366 0366
fax: 07 3366 0377

ACKNOWLEDGEMENTS

The authors and Publishers would like to thank Sacha Cohen and Ron Barber for all their hard work in the studio.

Paints supplied by
Crown Paints, Crown Decorative Products Ltd, PO Box 37, Crown House, Hollins Road, Darwen, Lancashire, BB30 B6
Specialist paints supplied by Paint Magic, 79 Shepperton Road, Islington, London, N1 3DF

INDEX